This Coloring Book Belongs To:

Color Chart

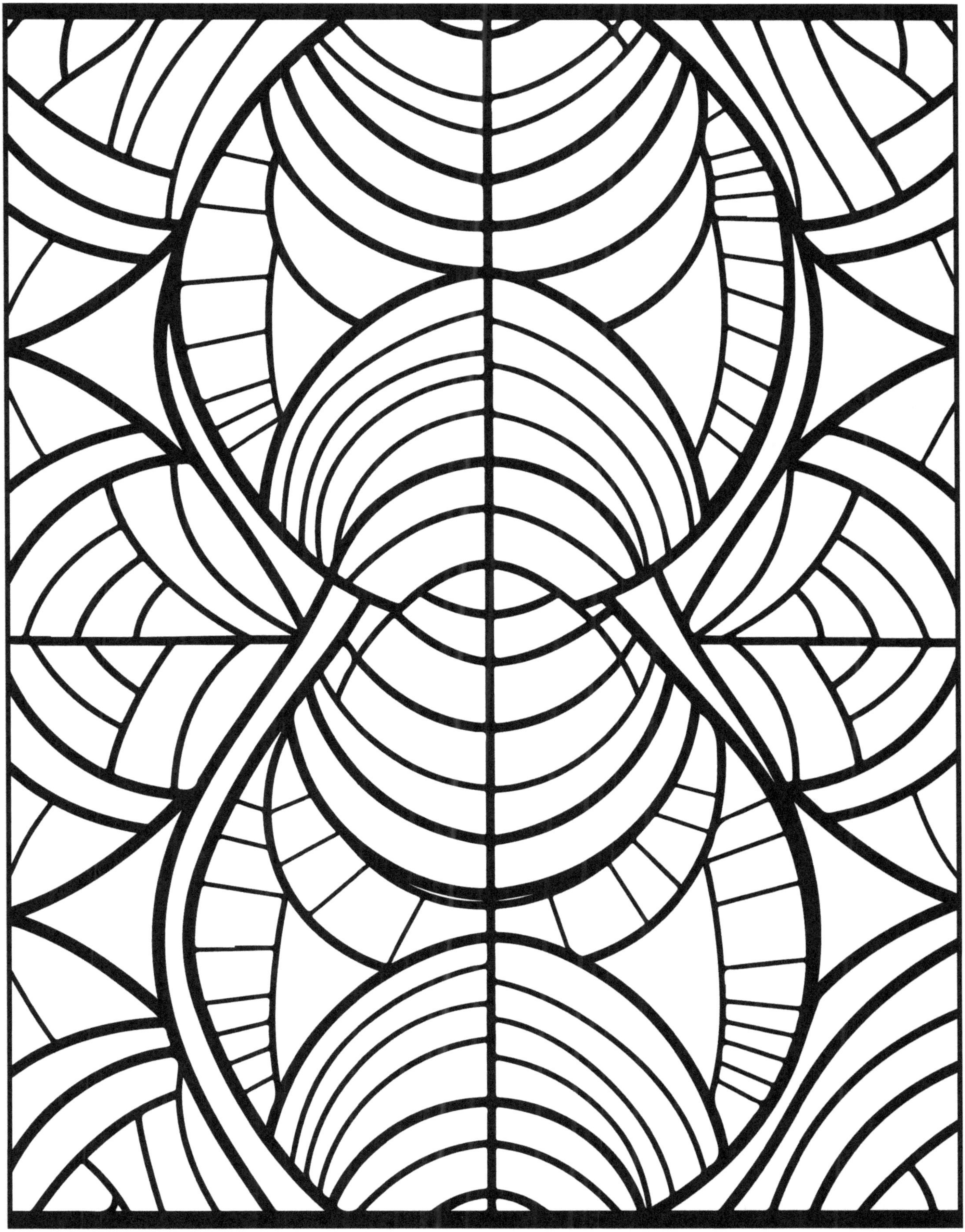

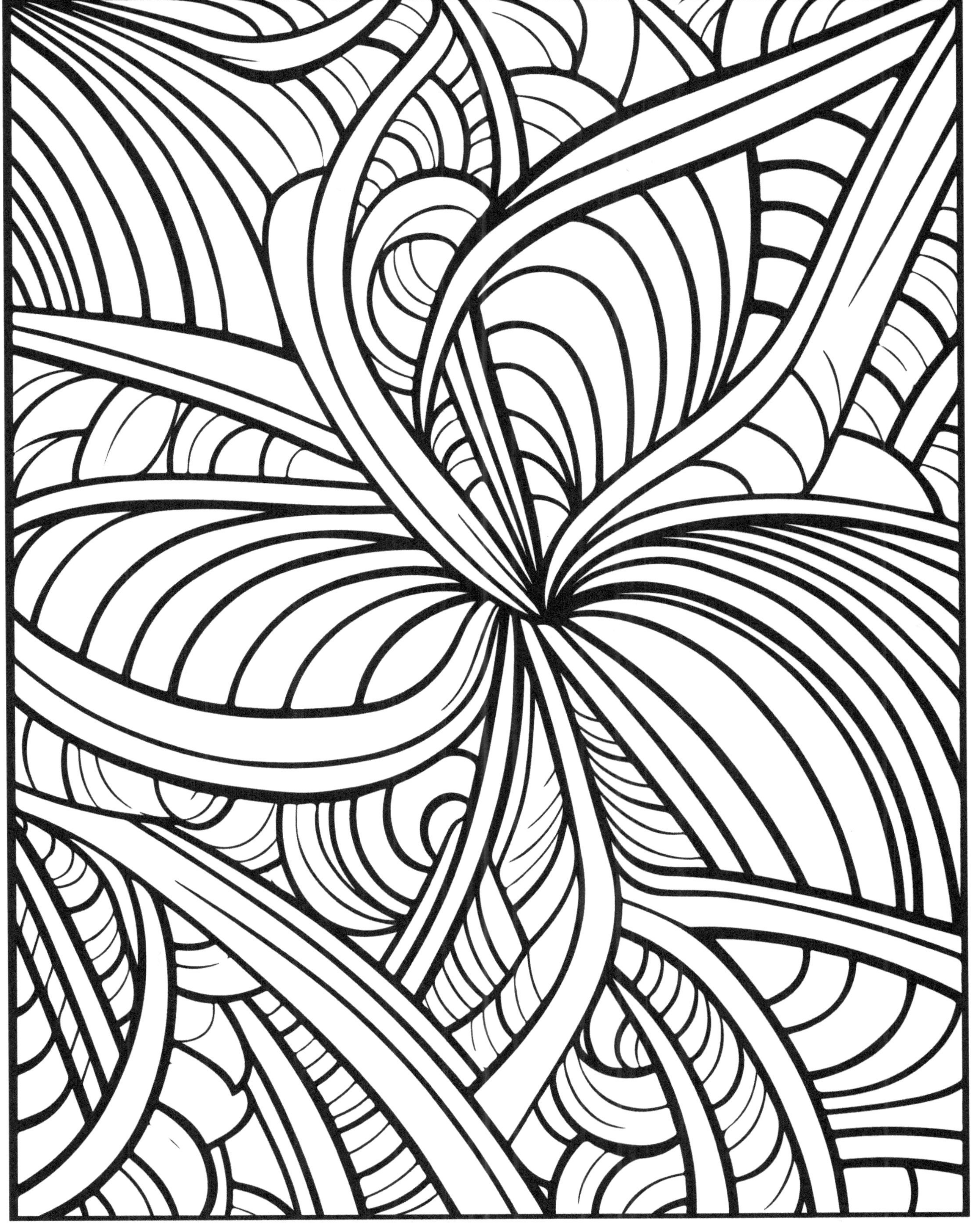

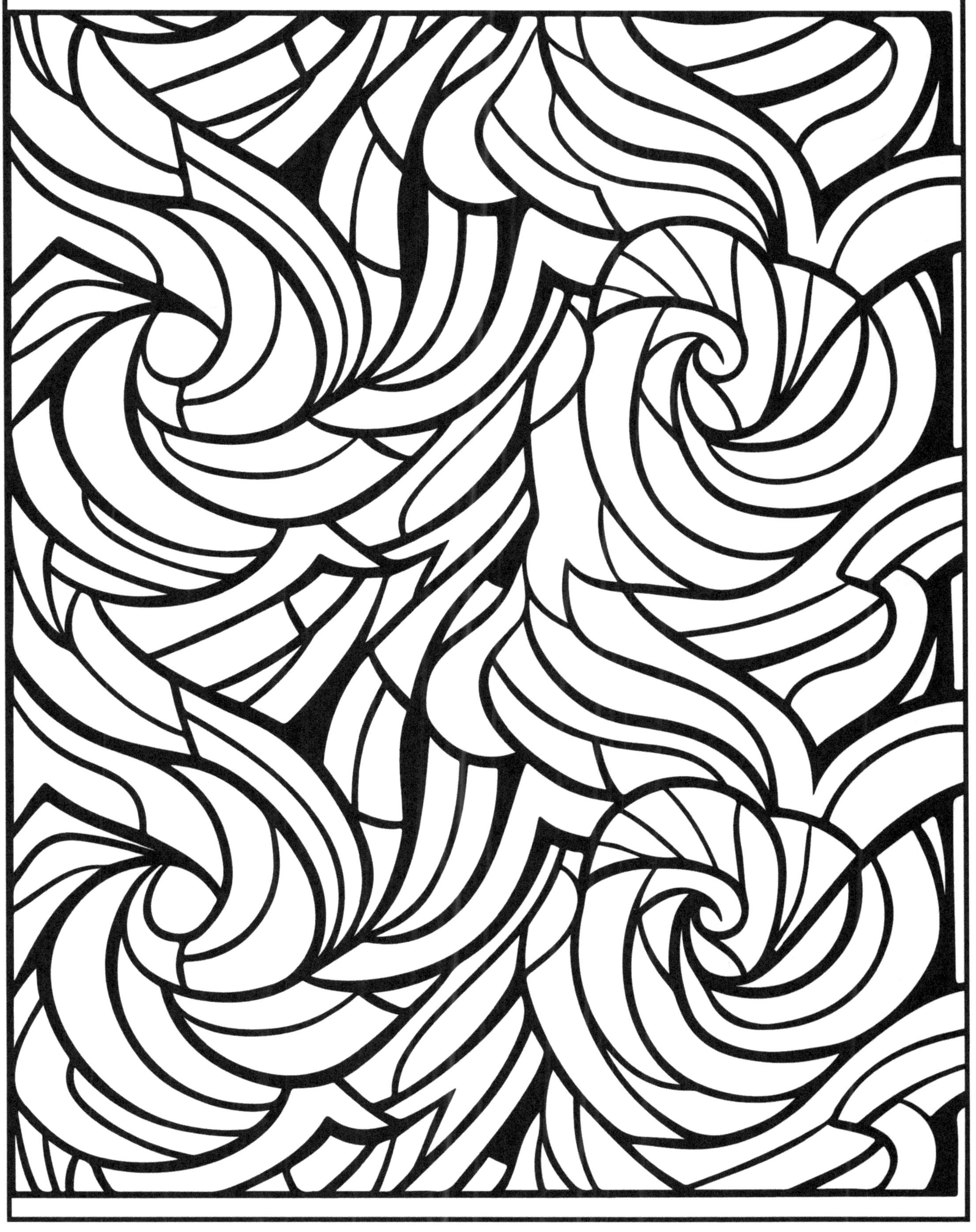

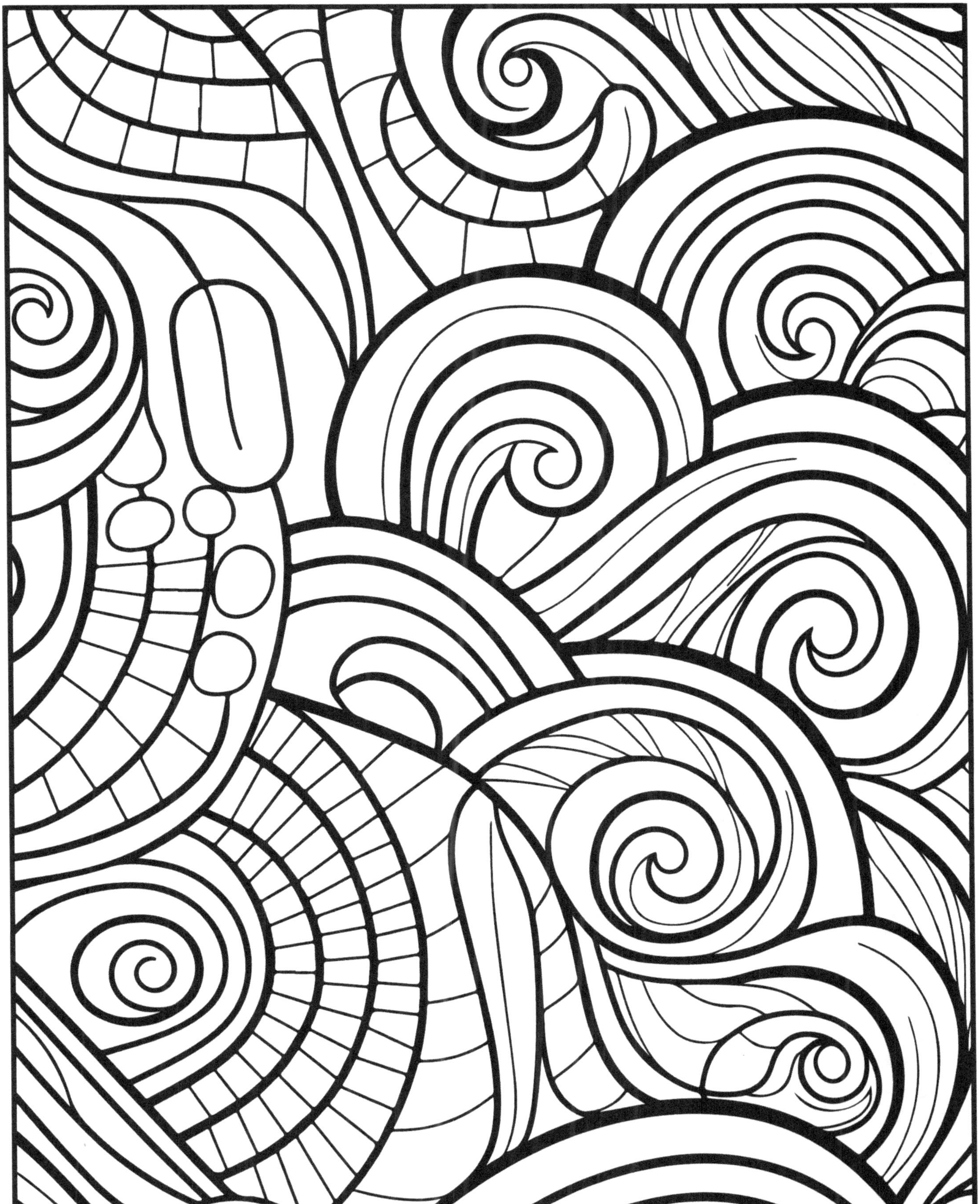

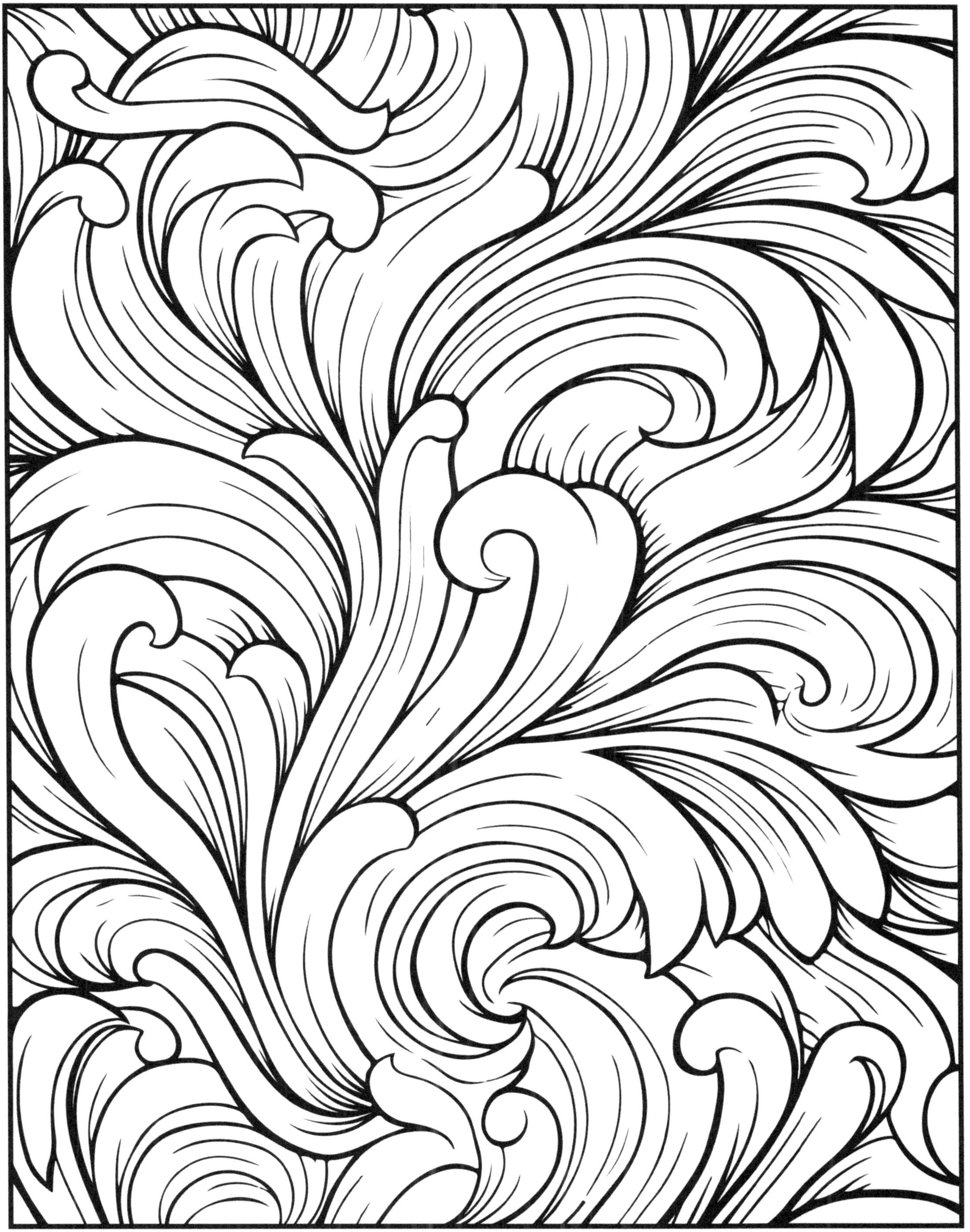

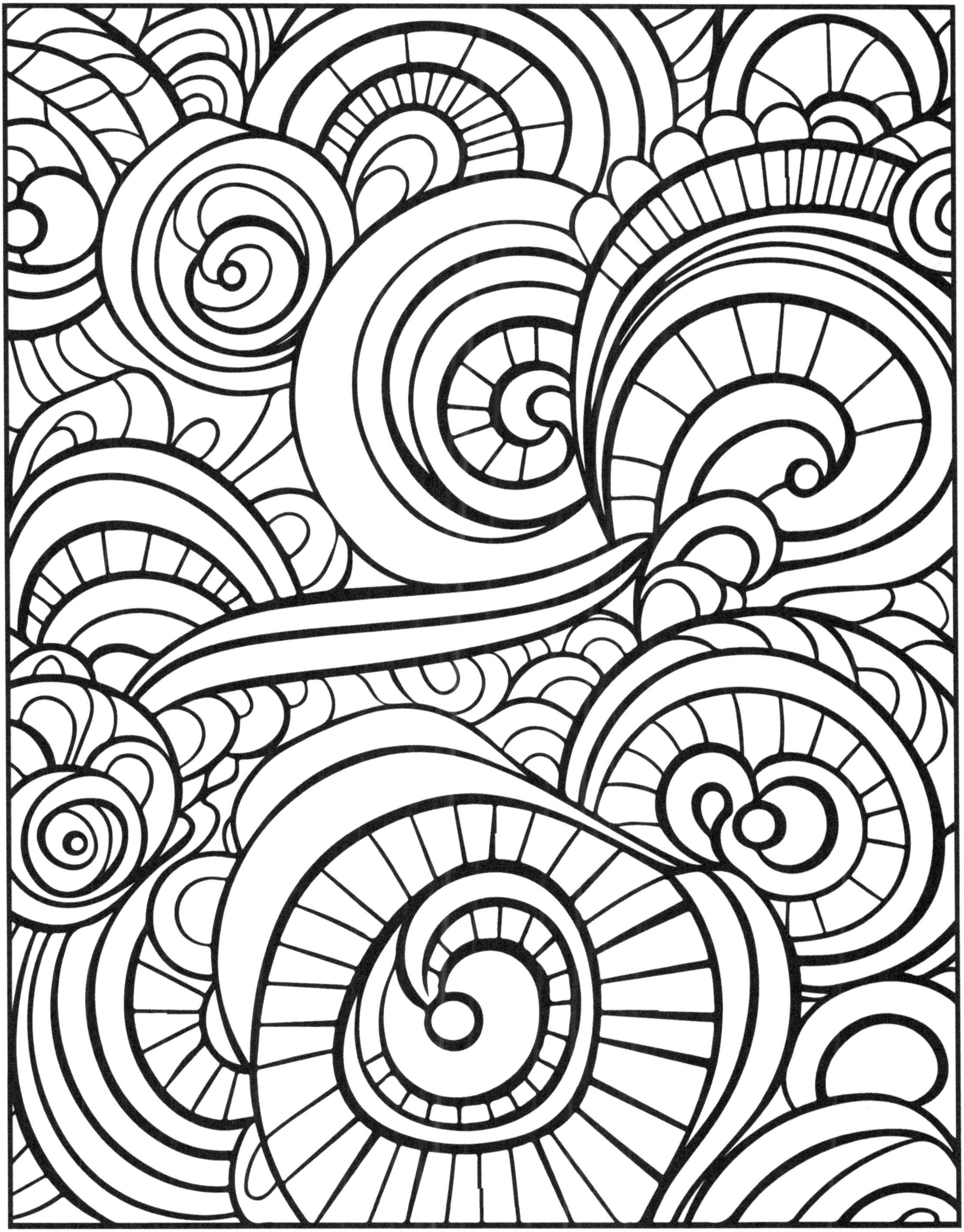

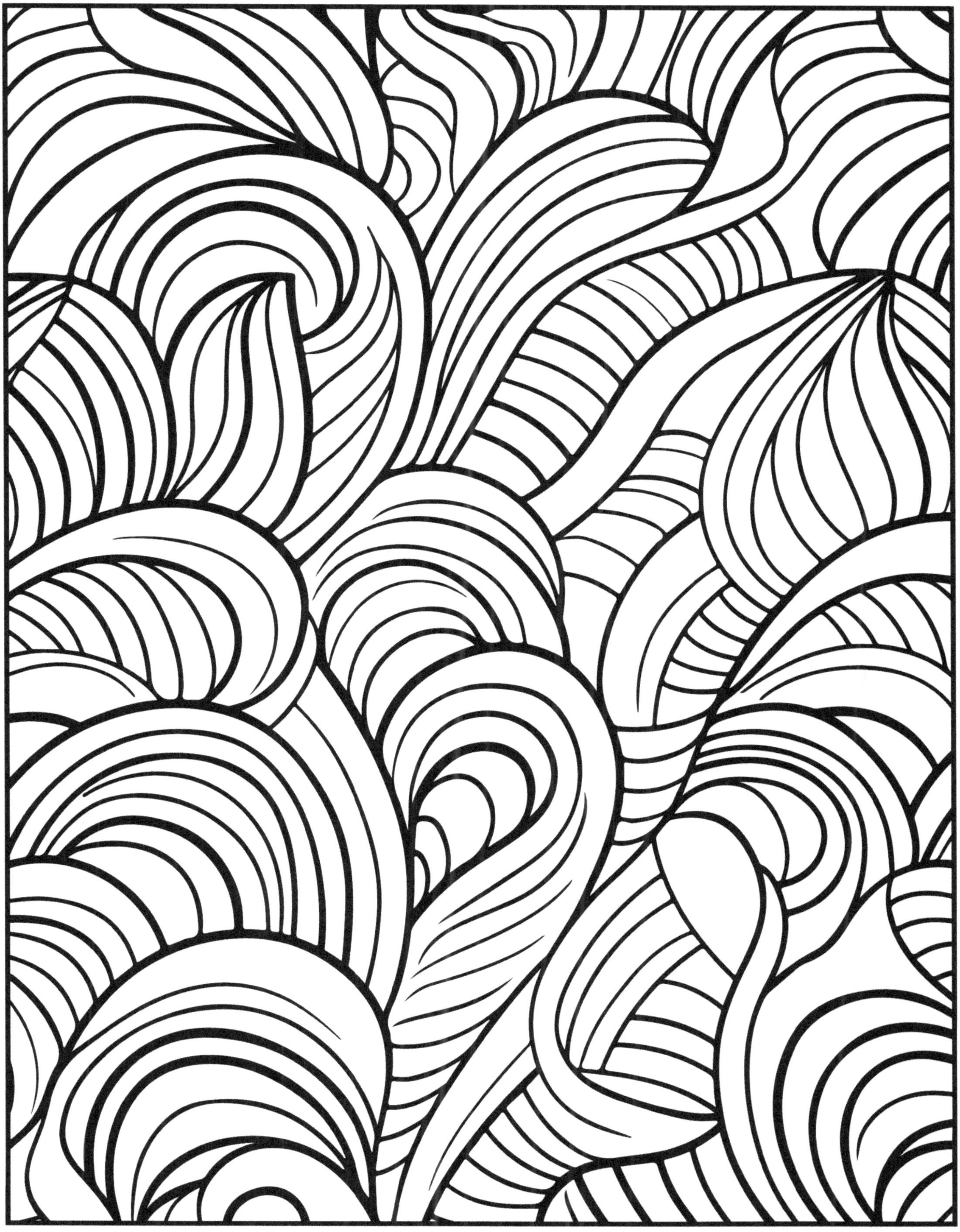

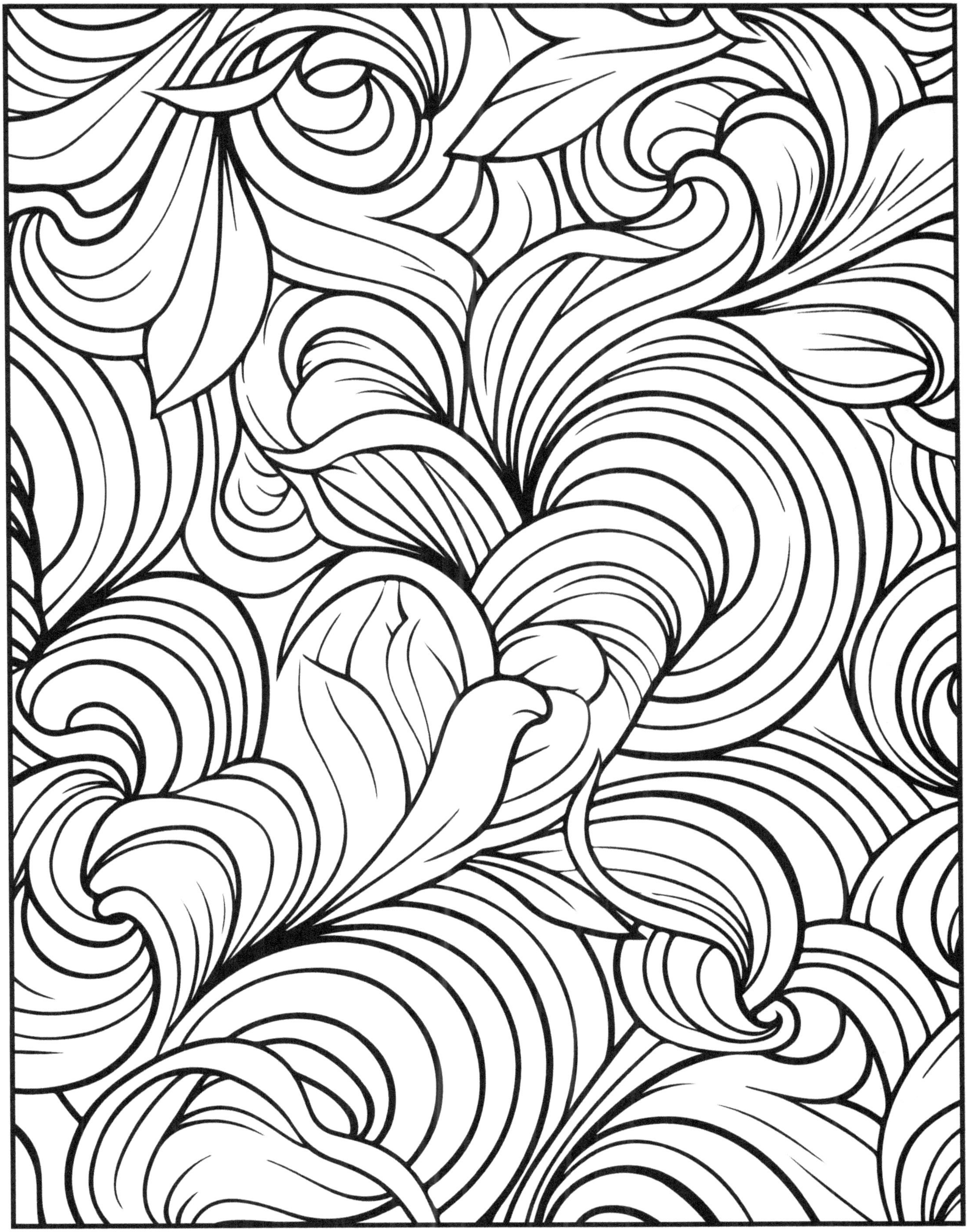

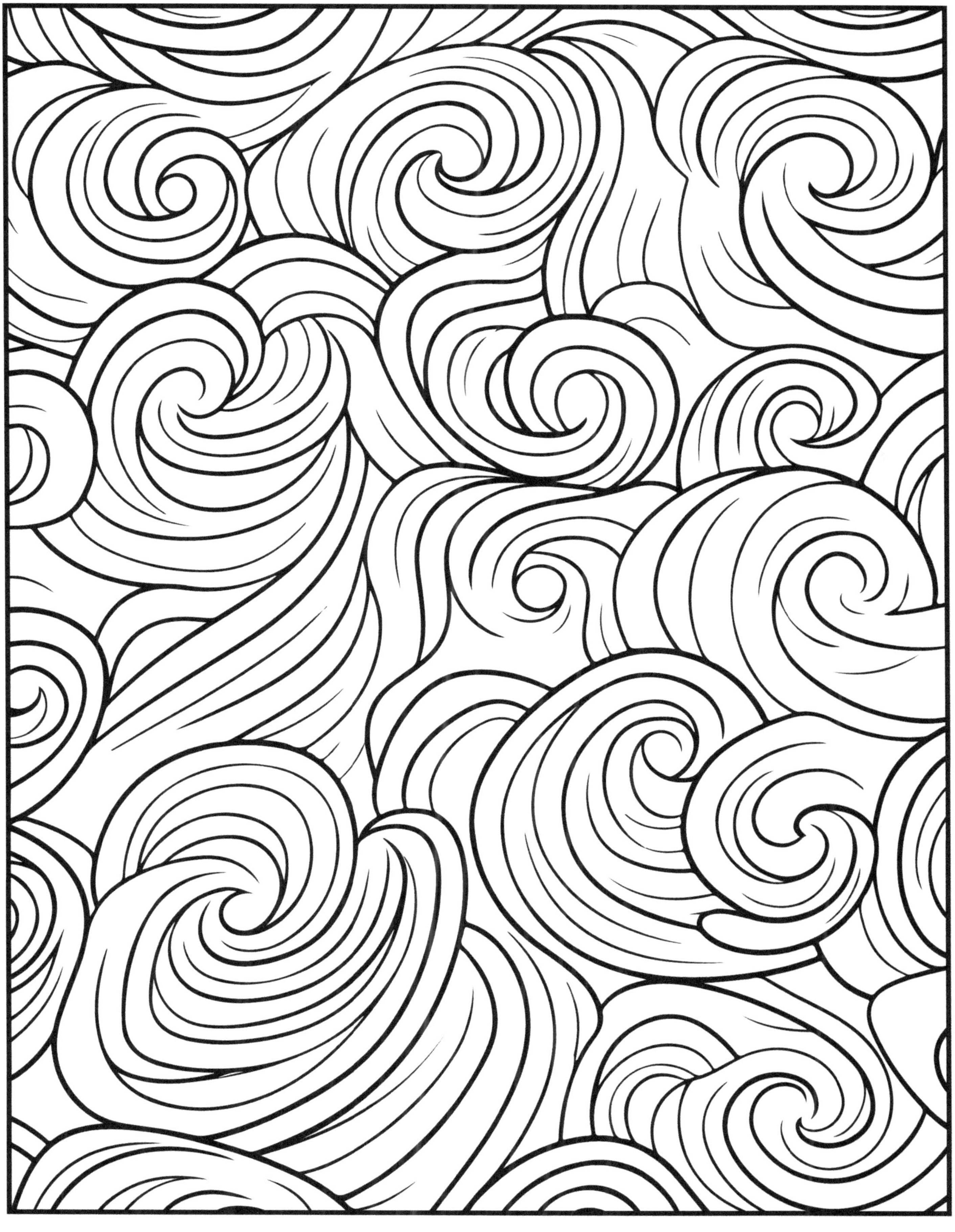

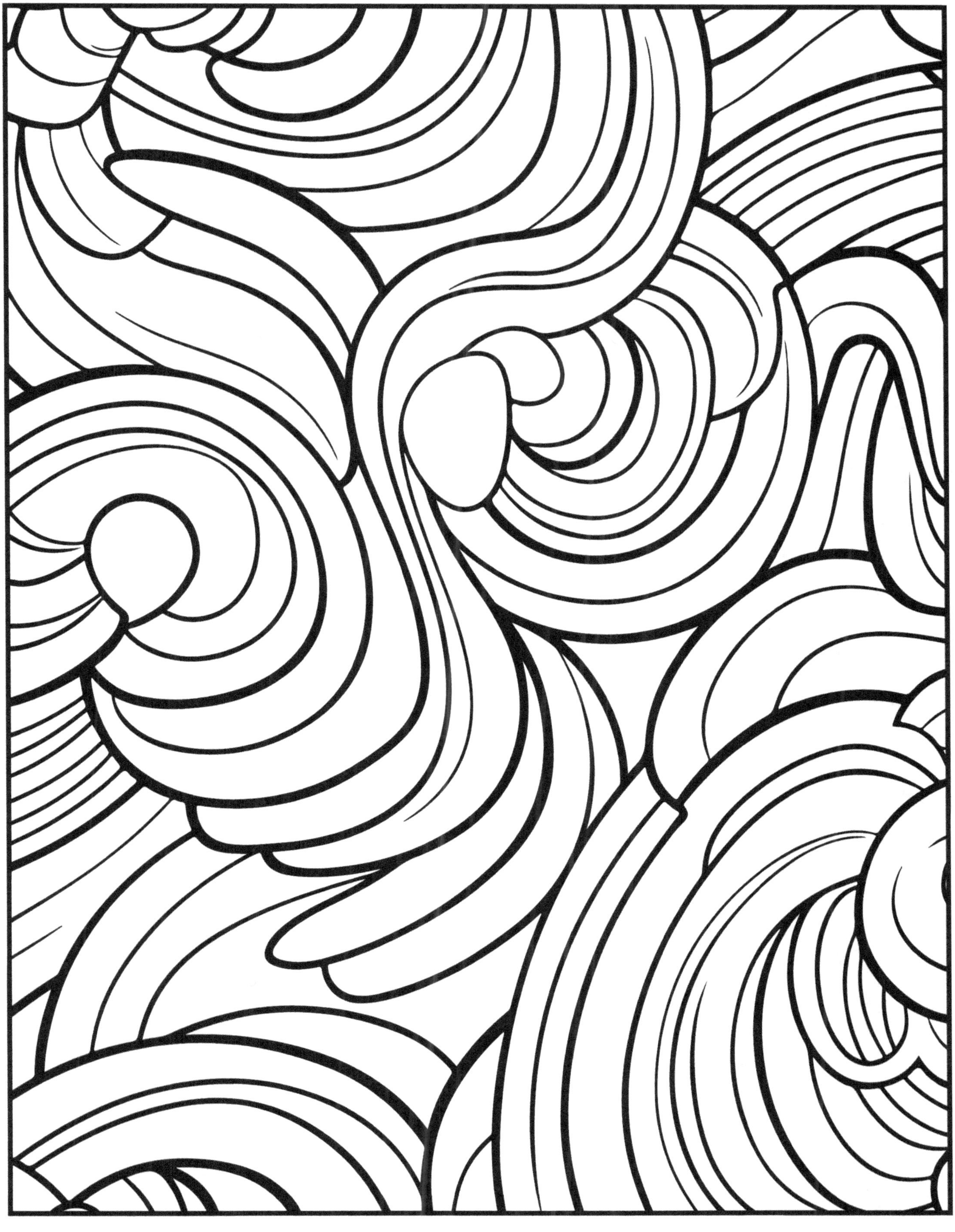

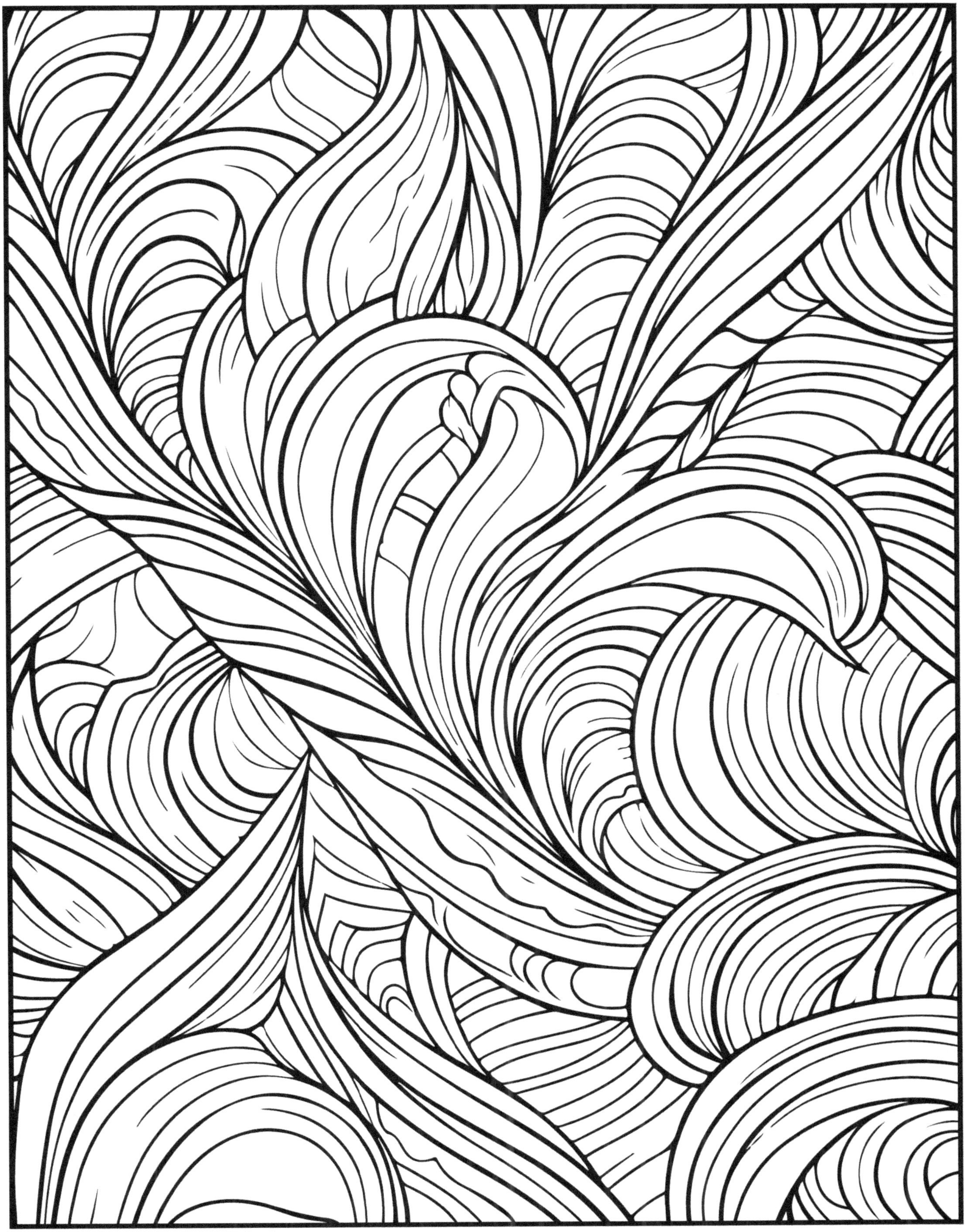

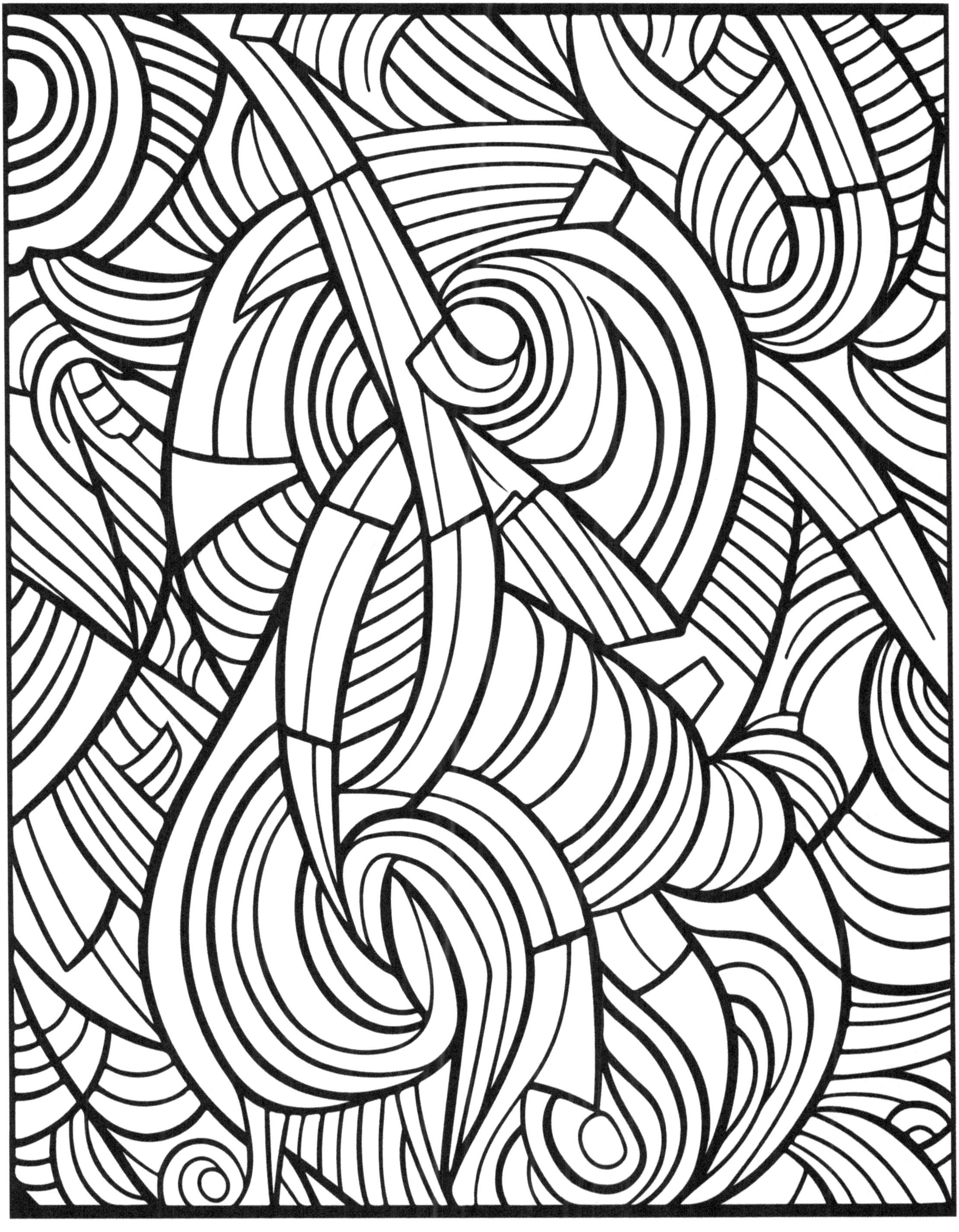

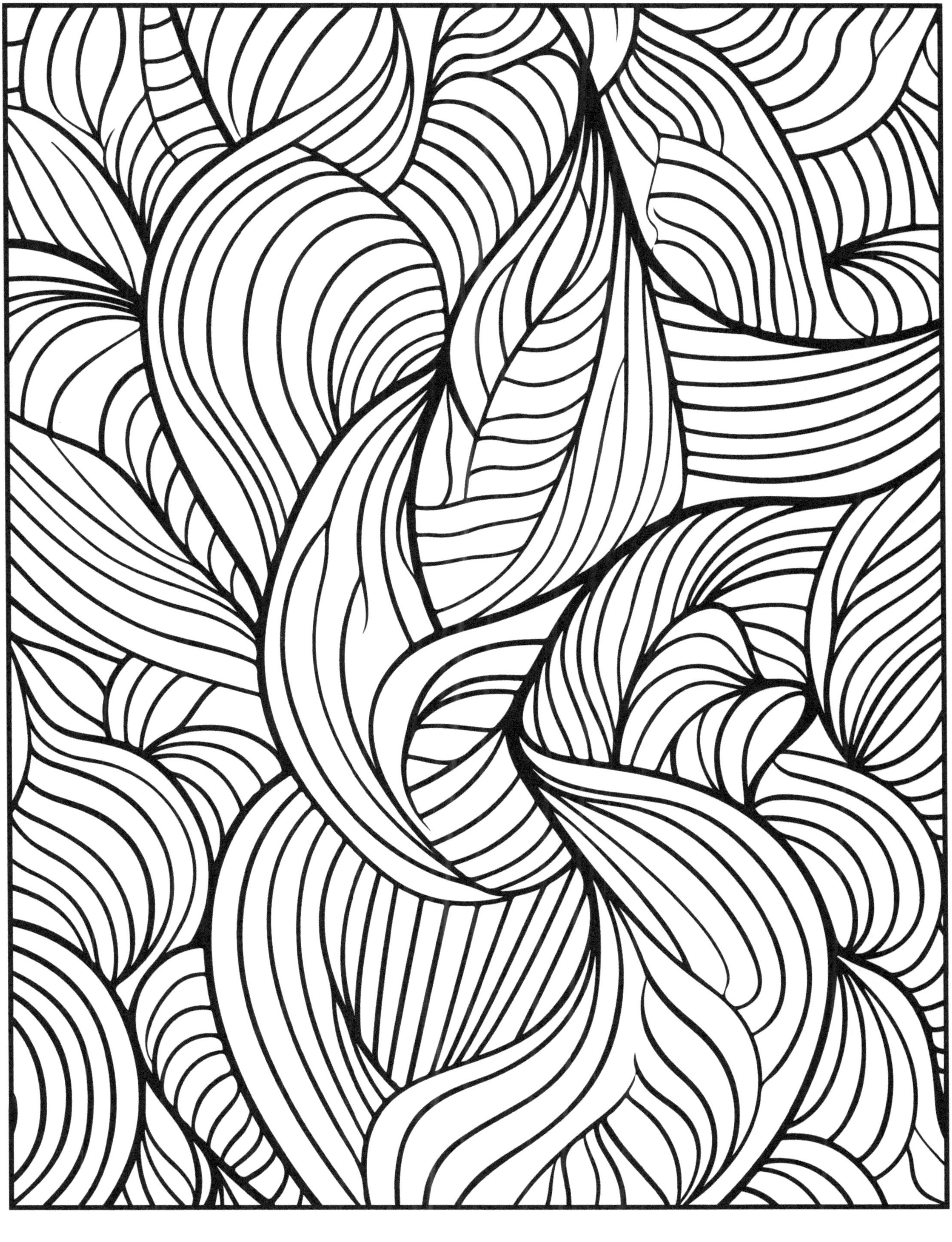

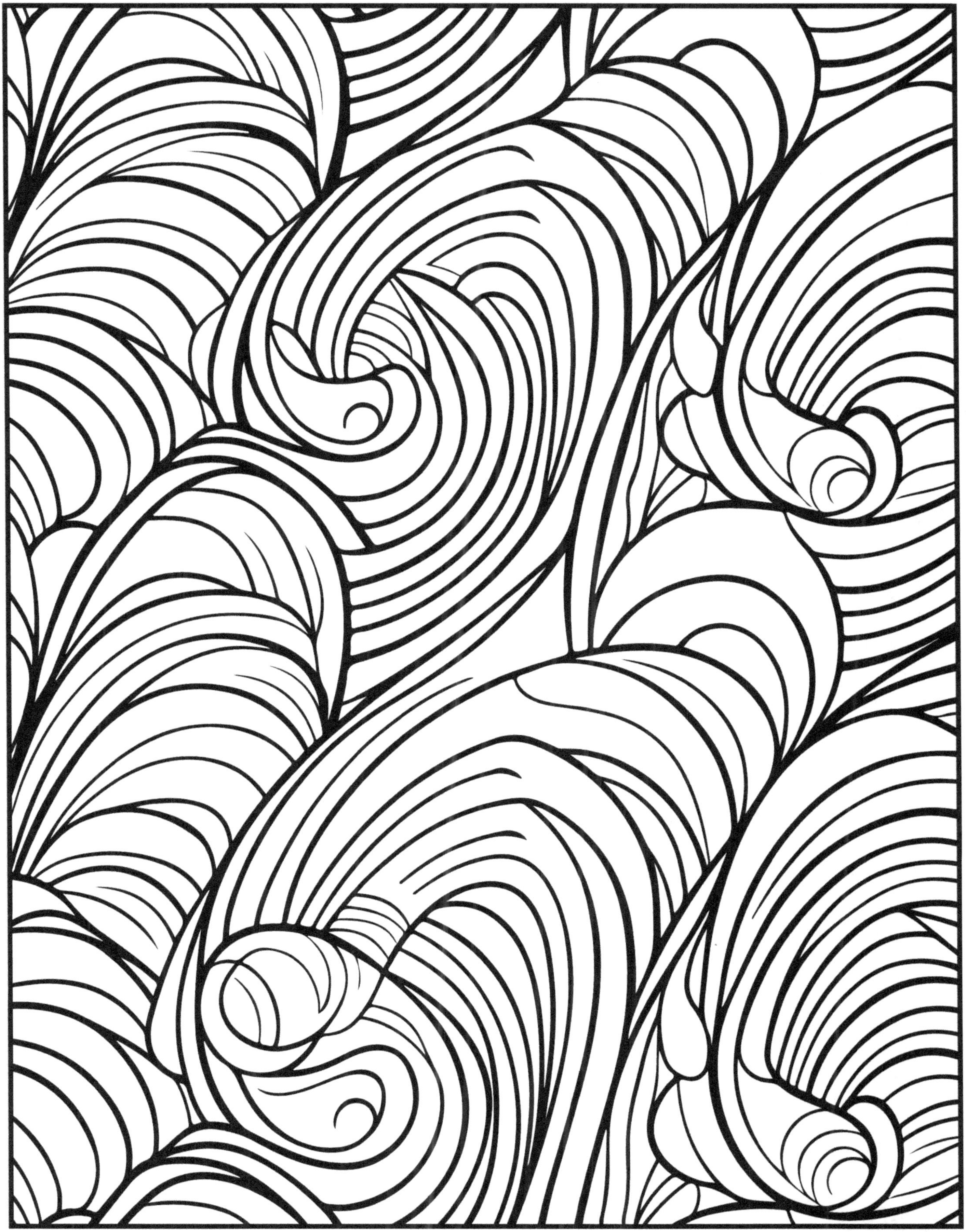

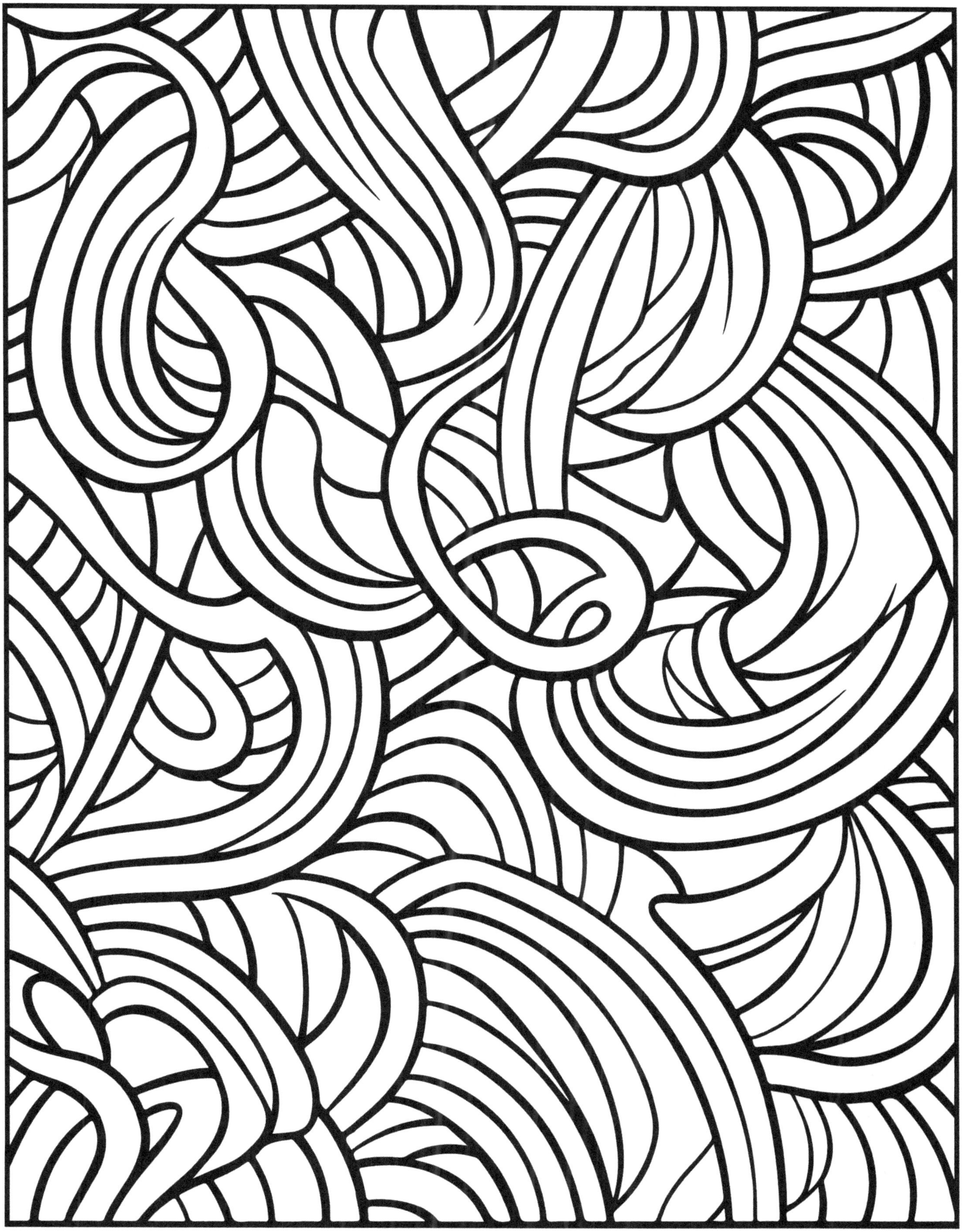

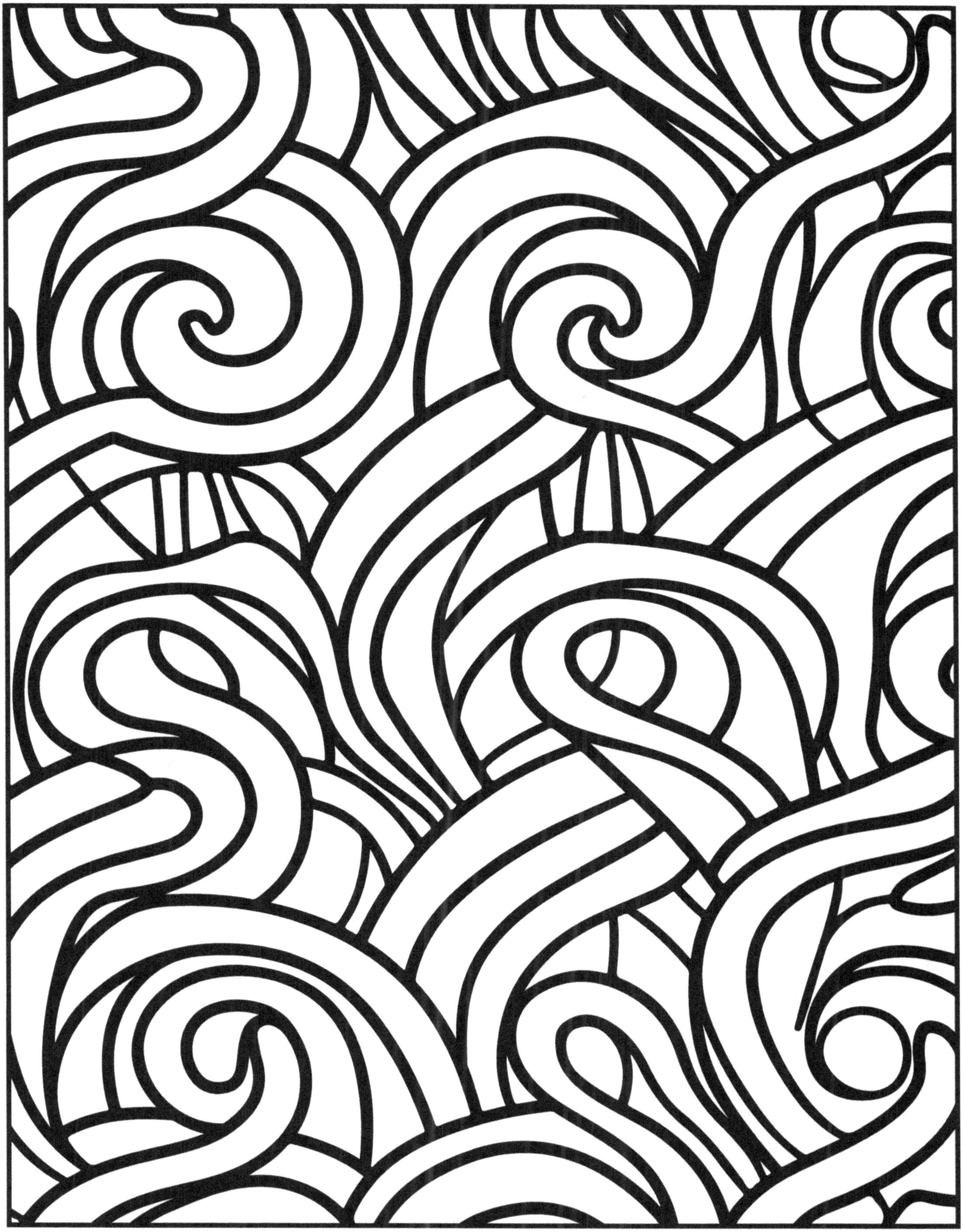

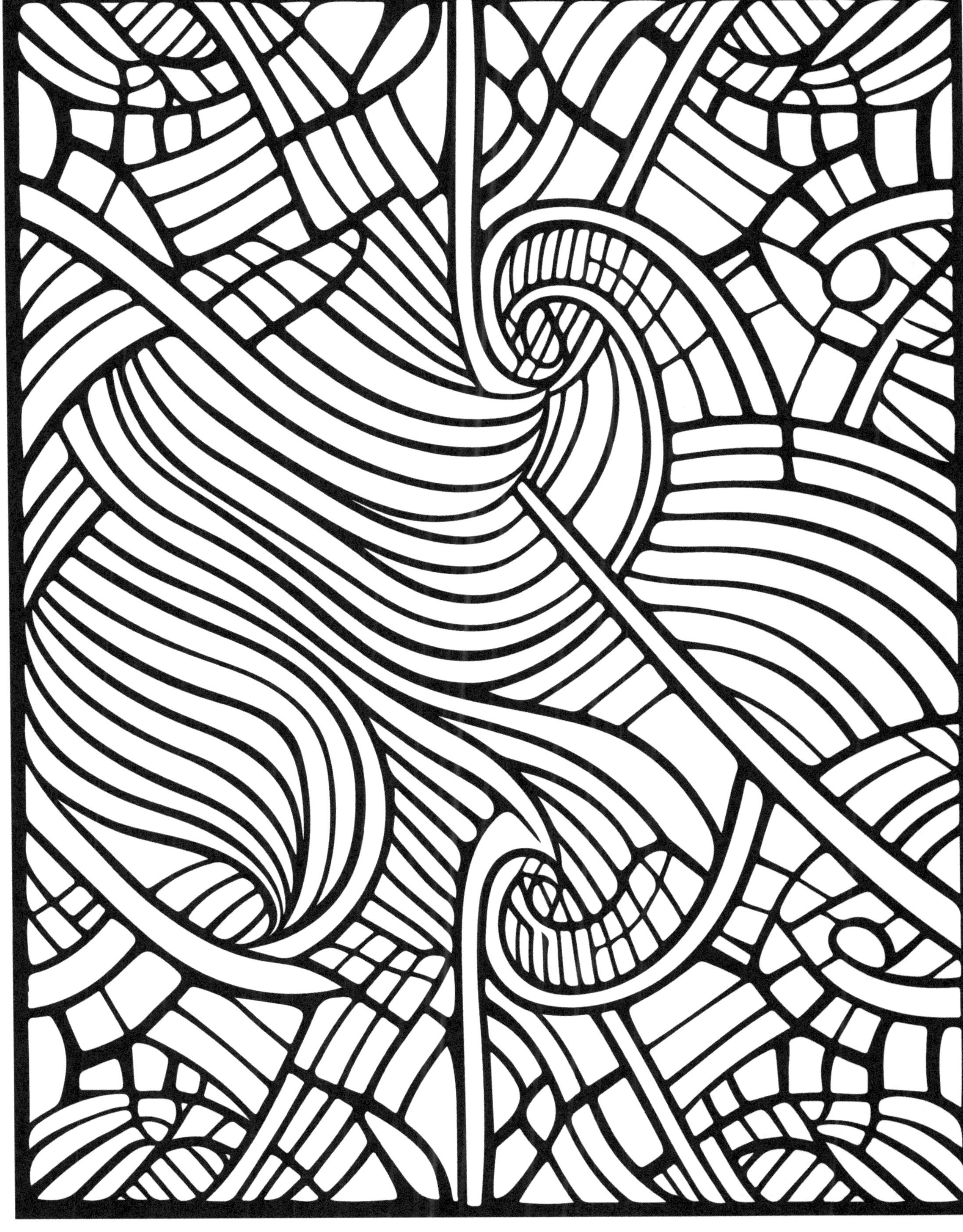

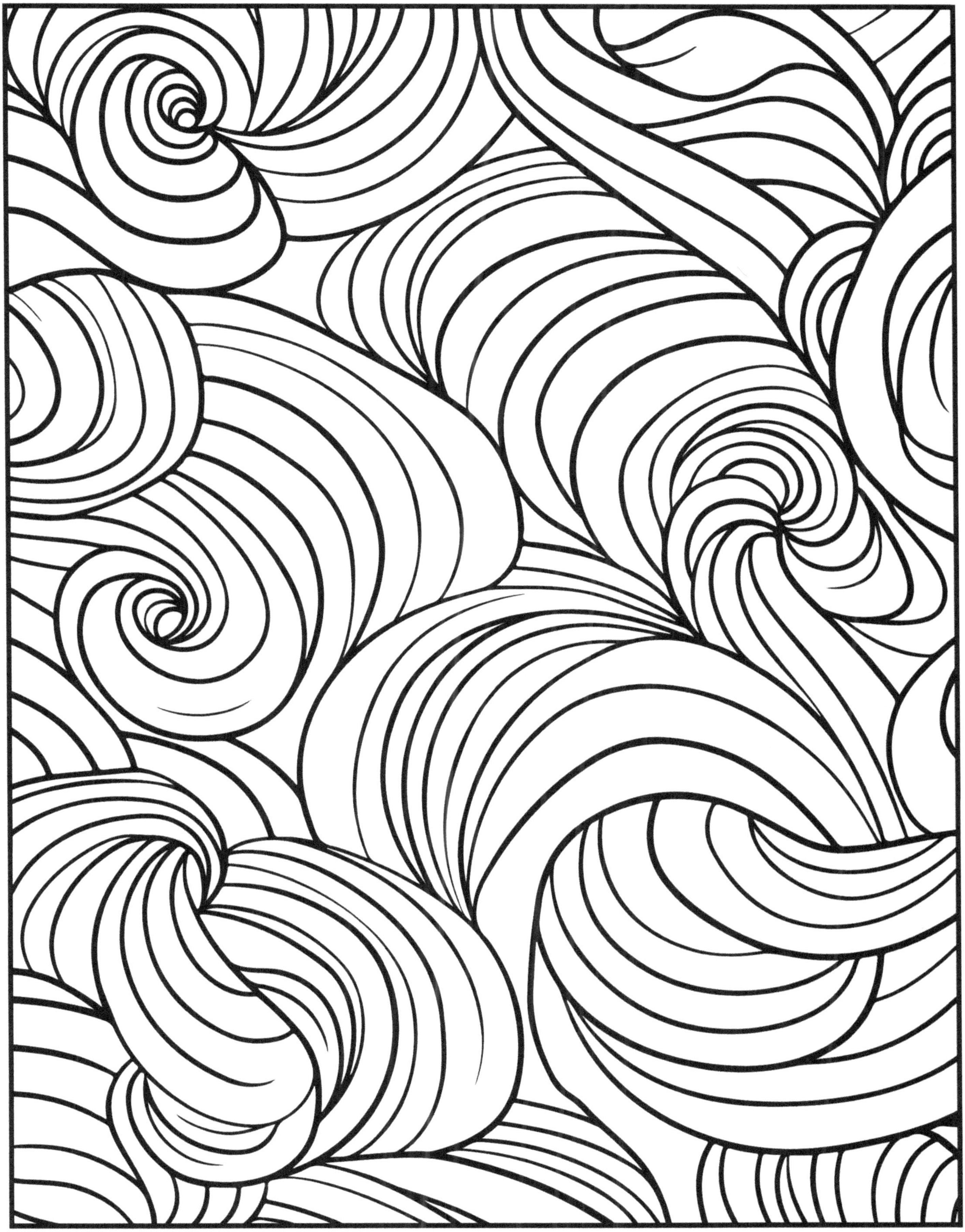

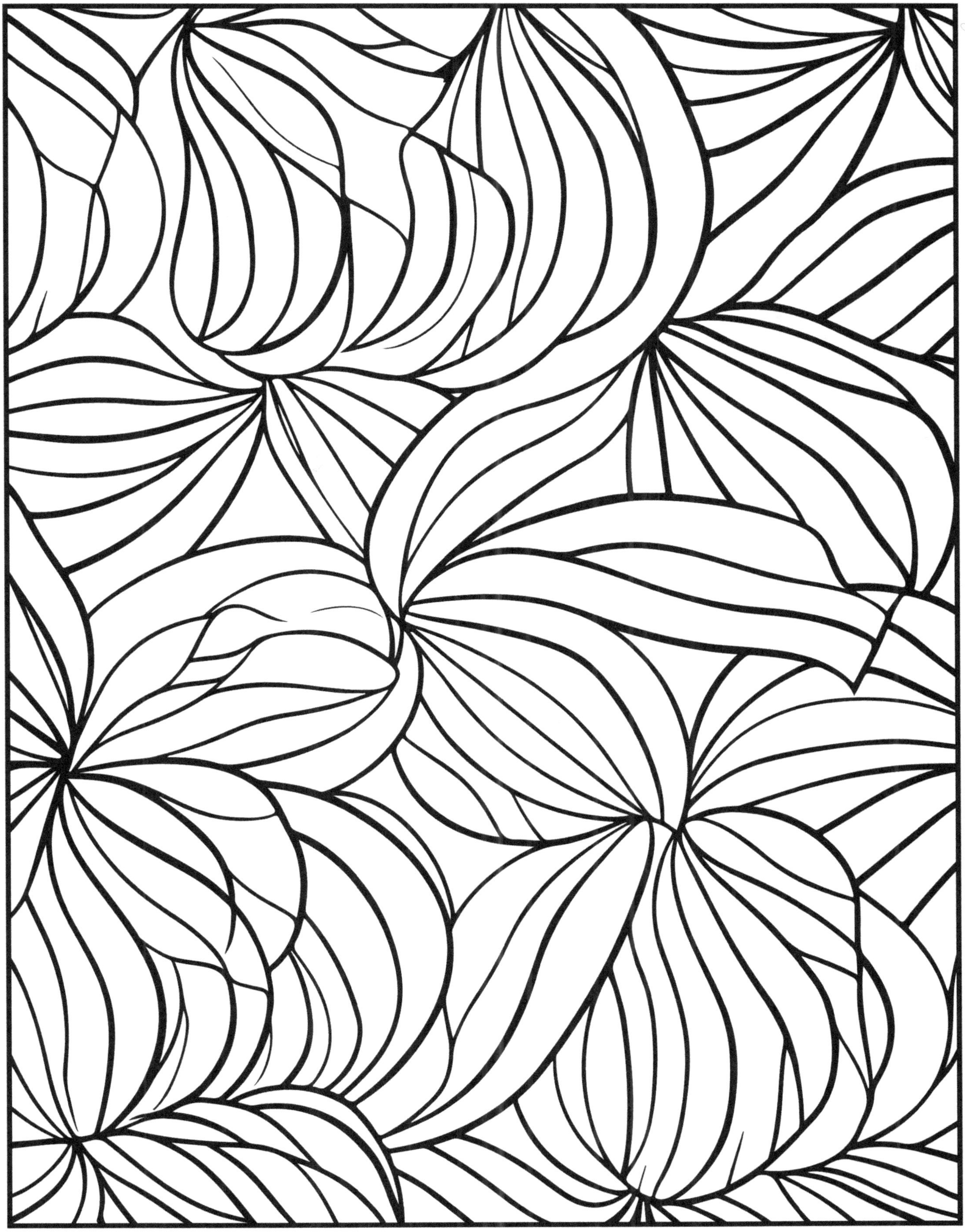

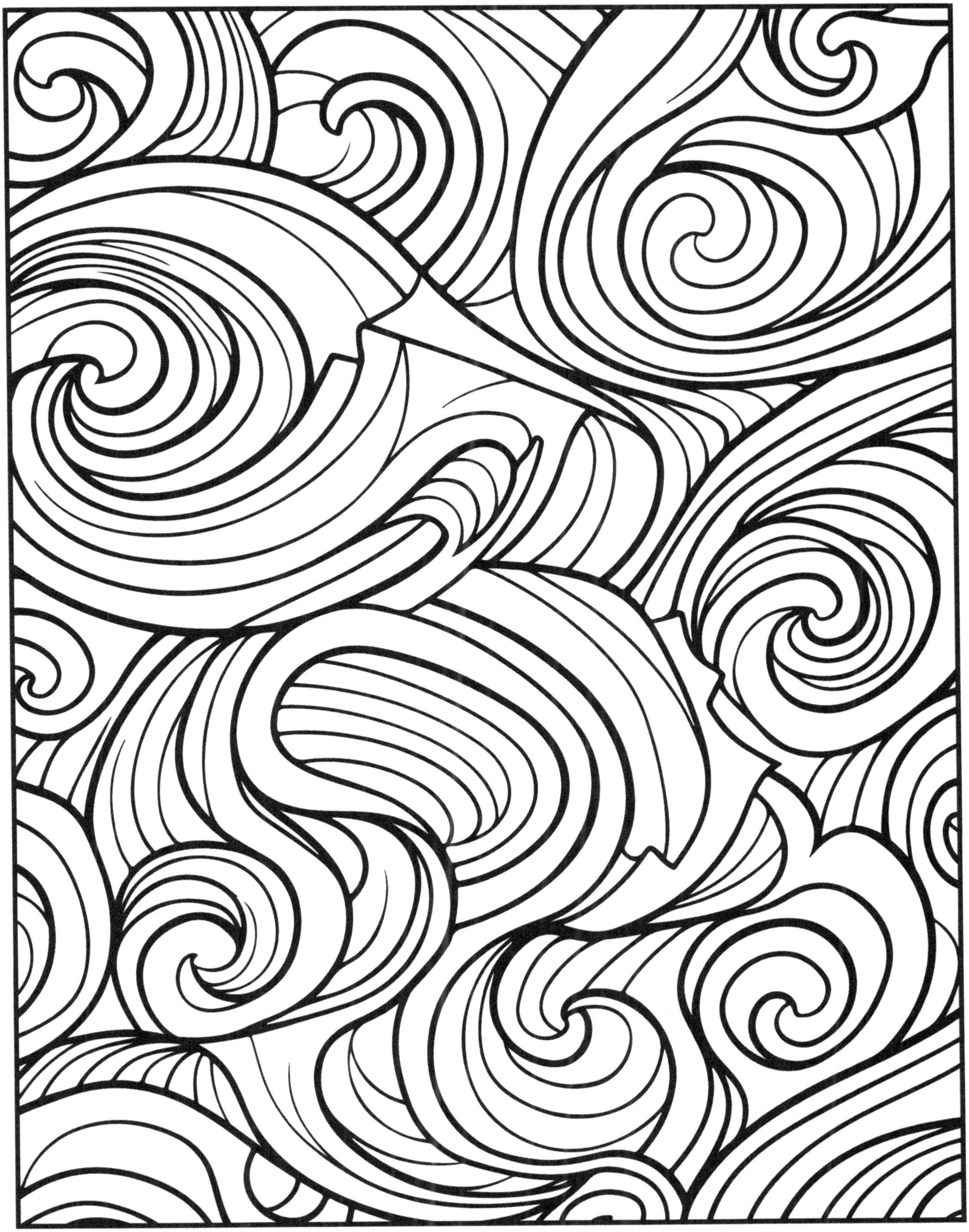

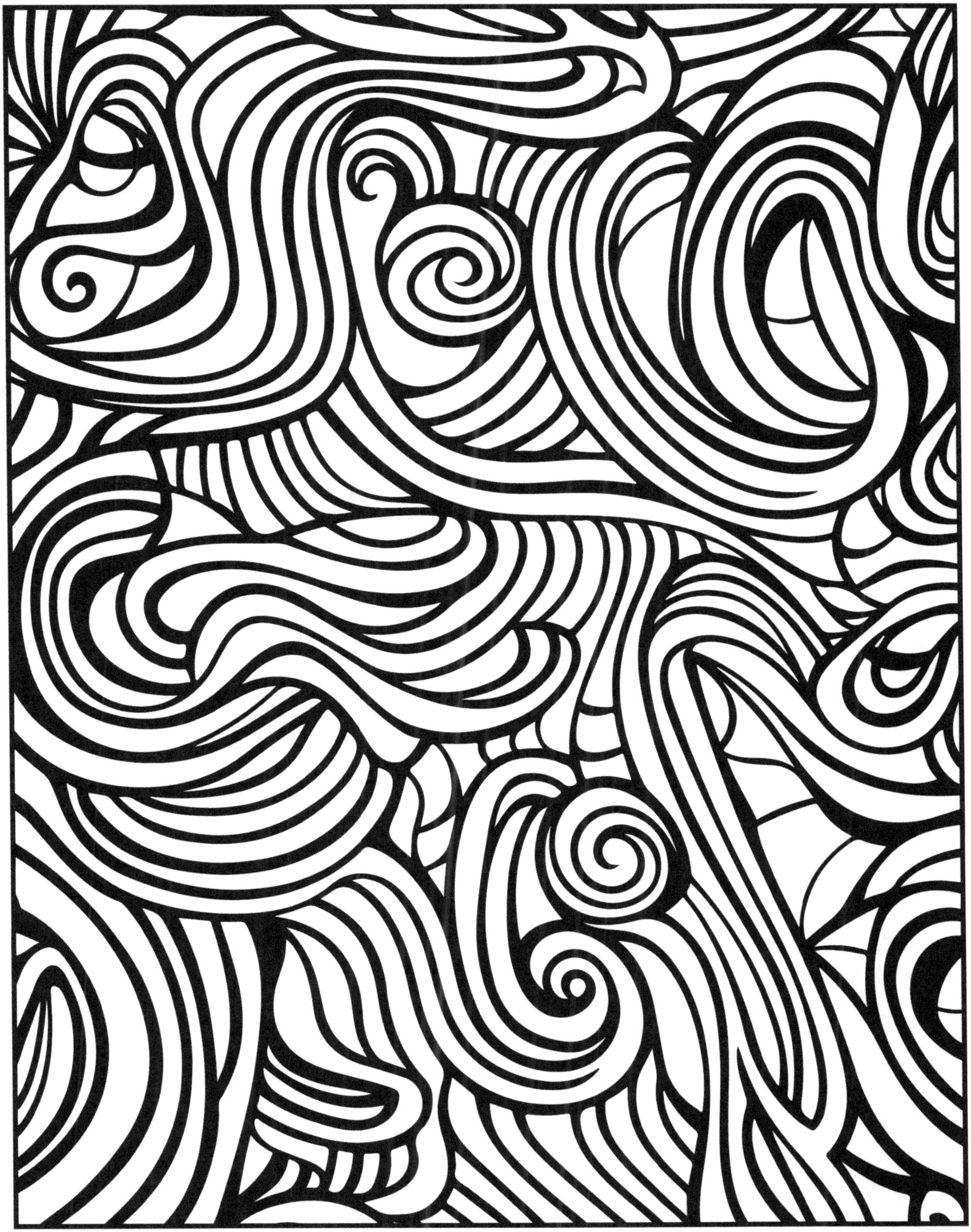

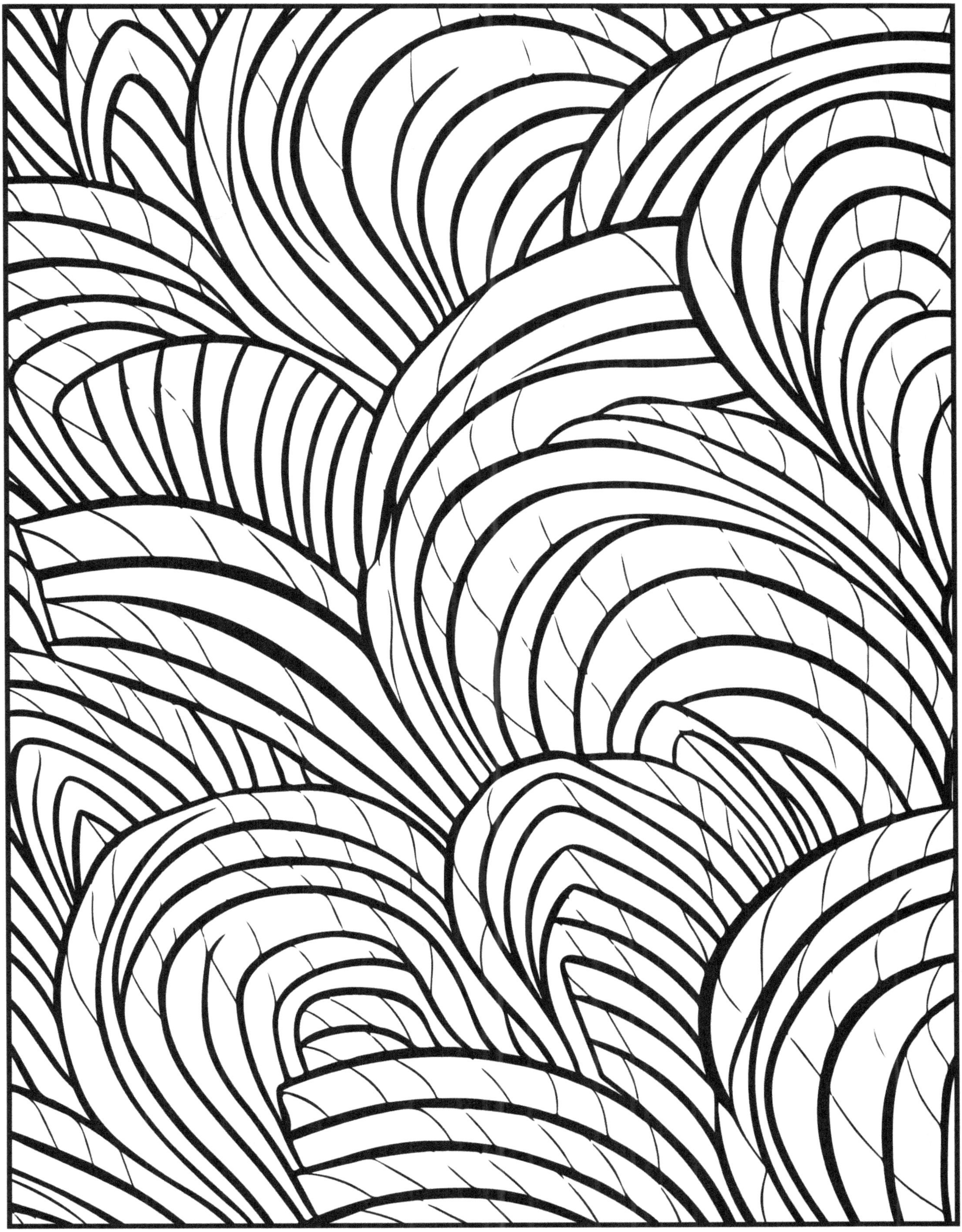

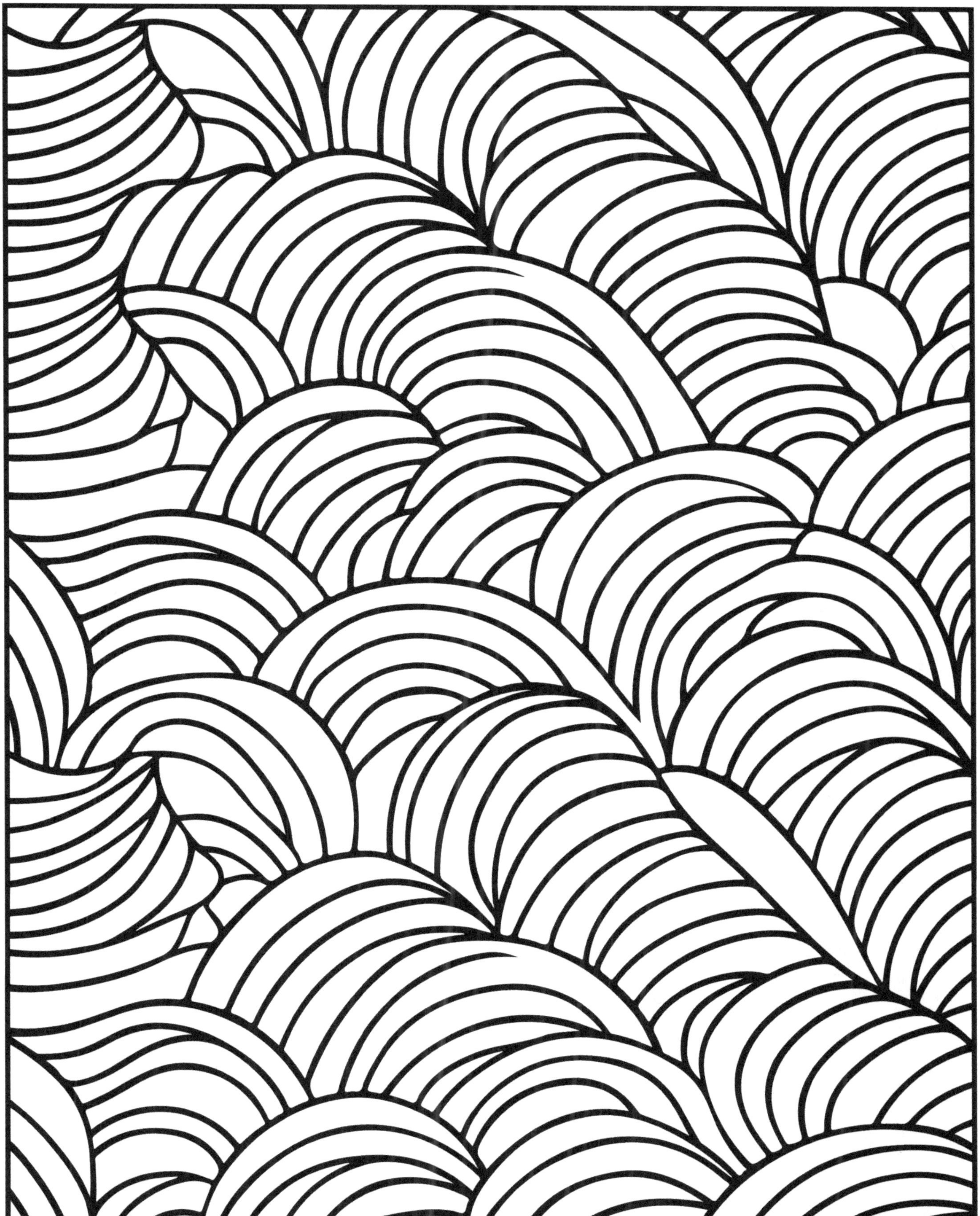

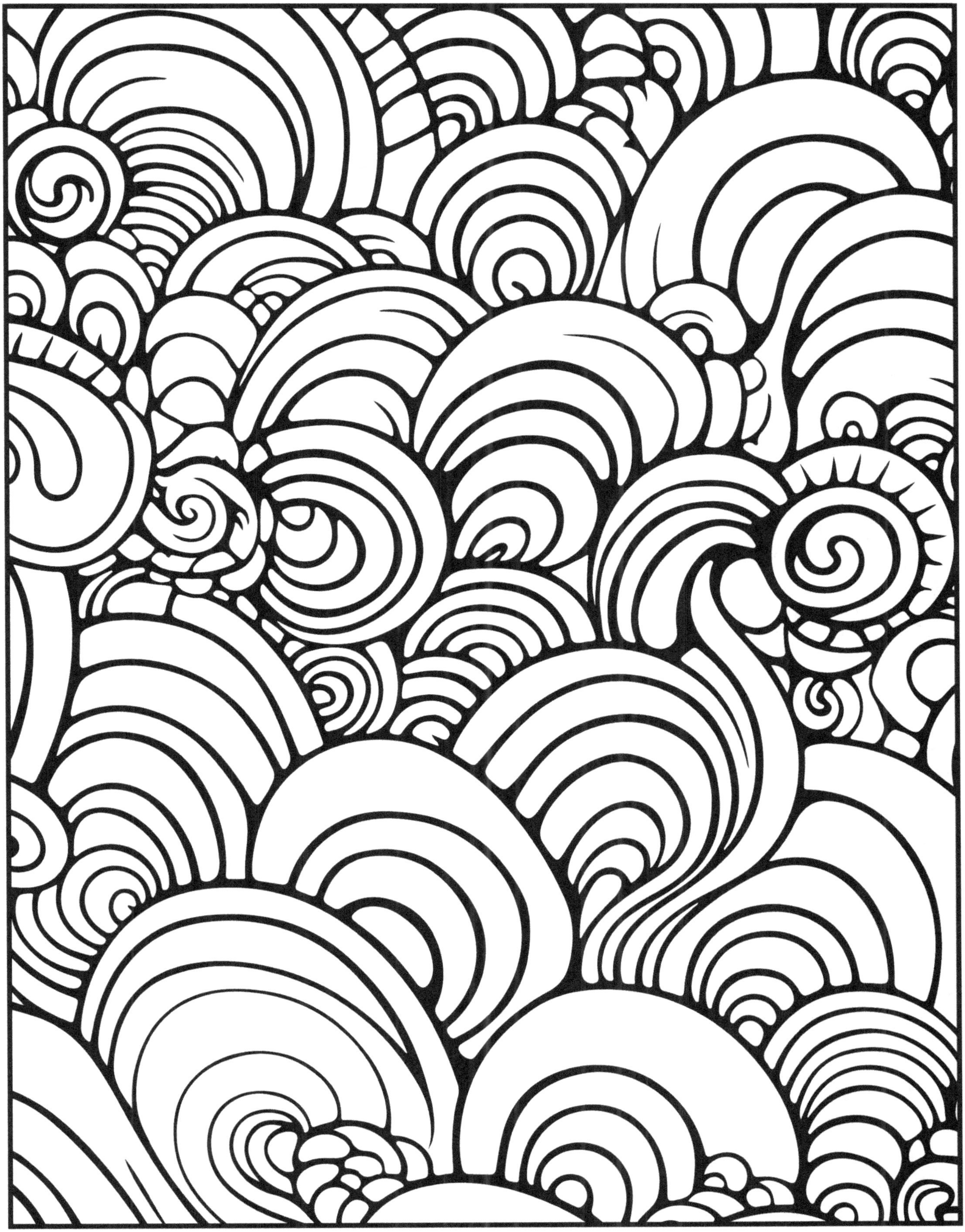

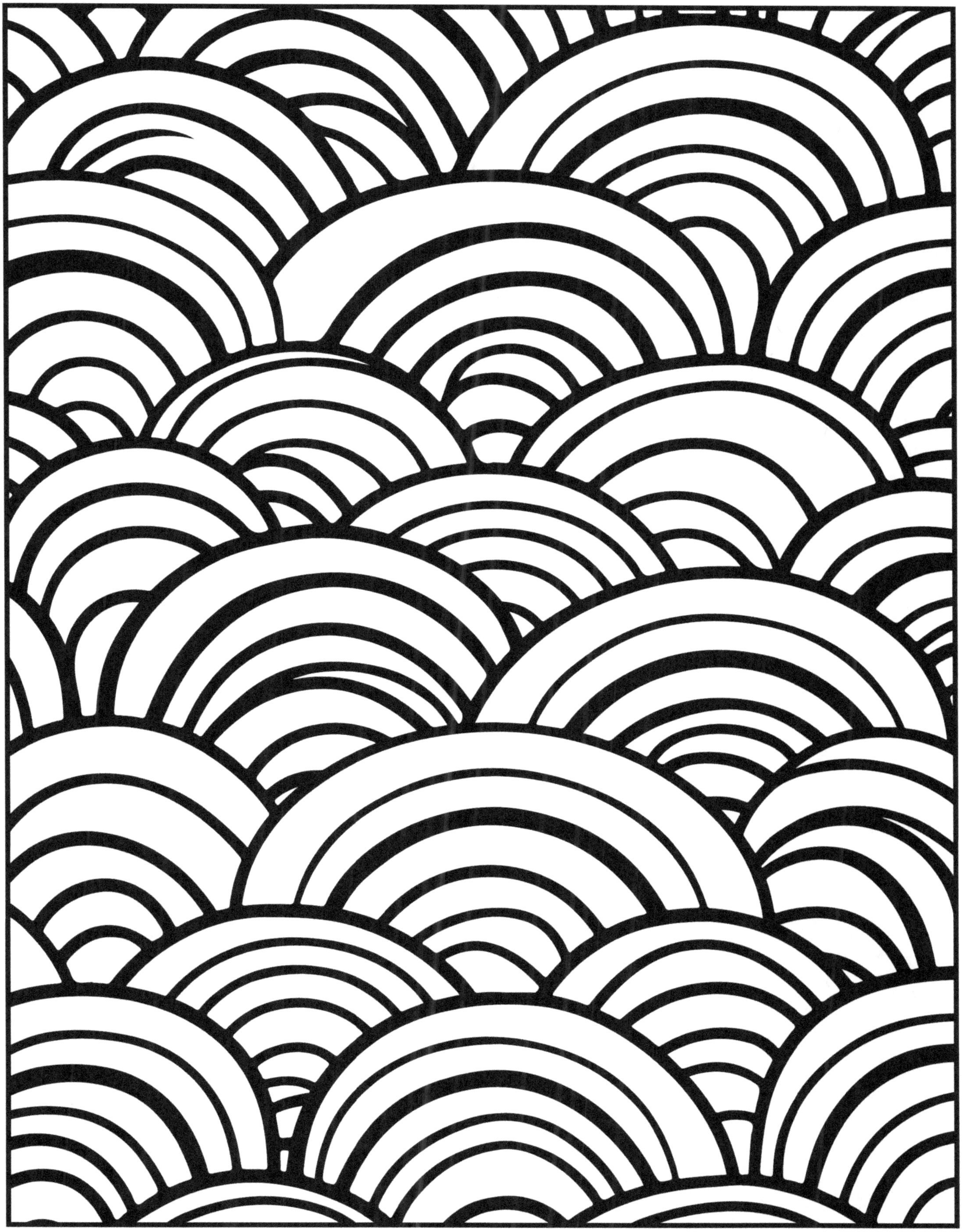

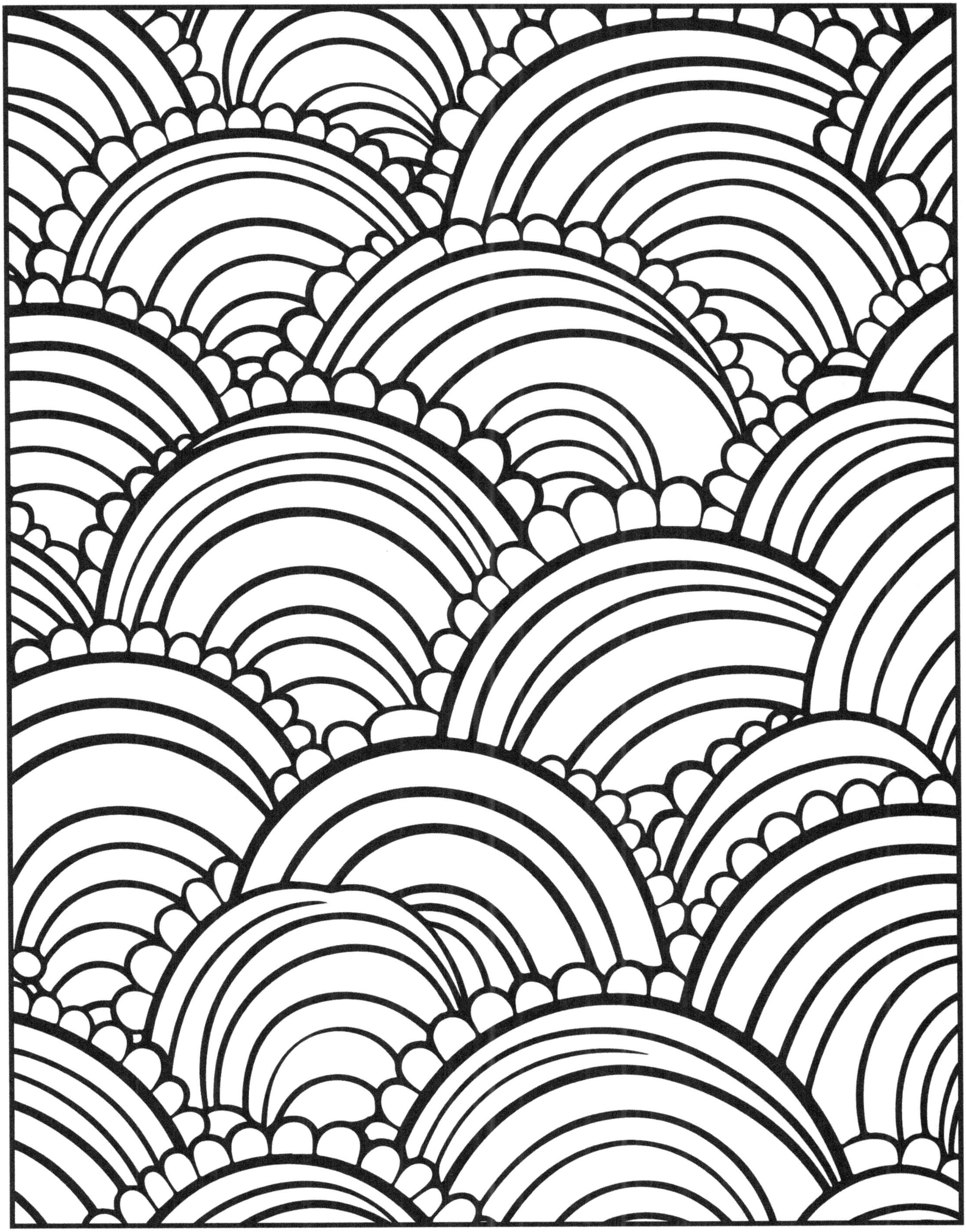

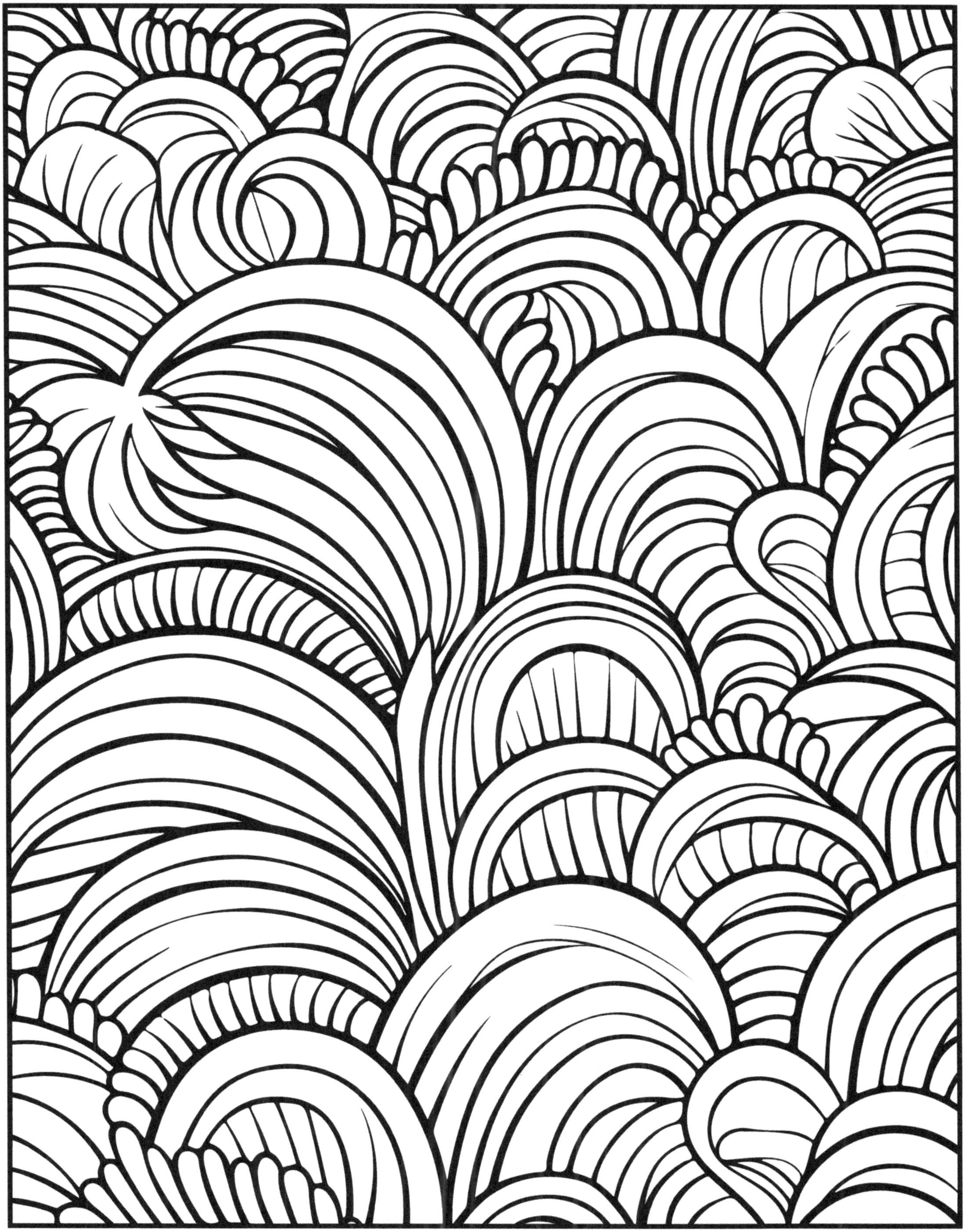

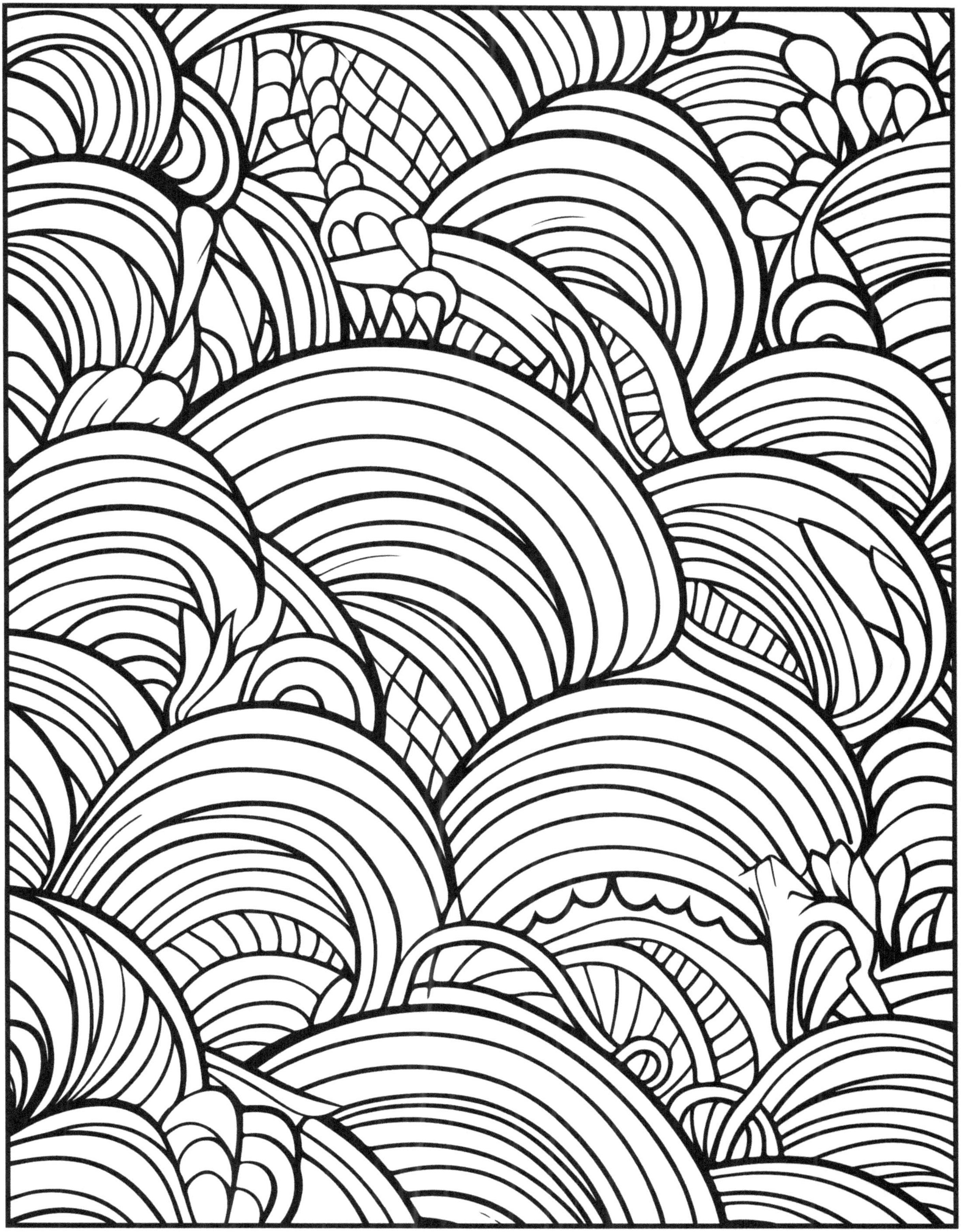

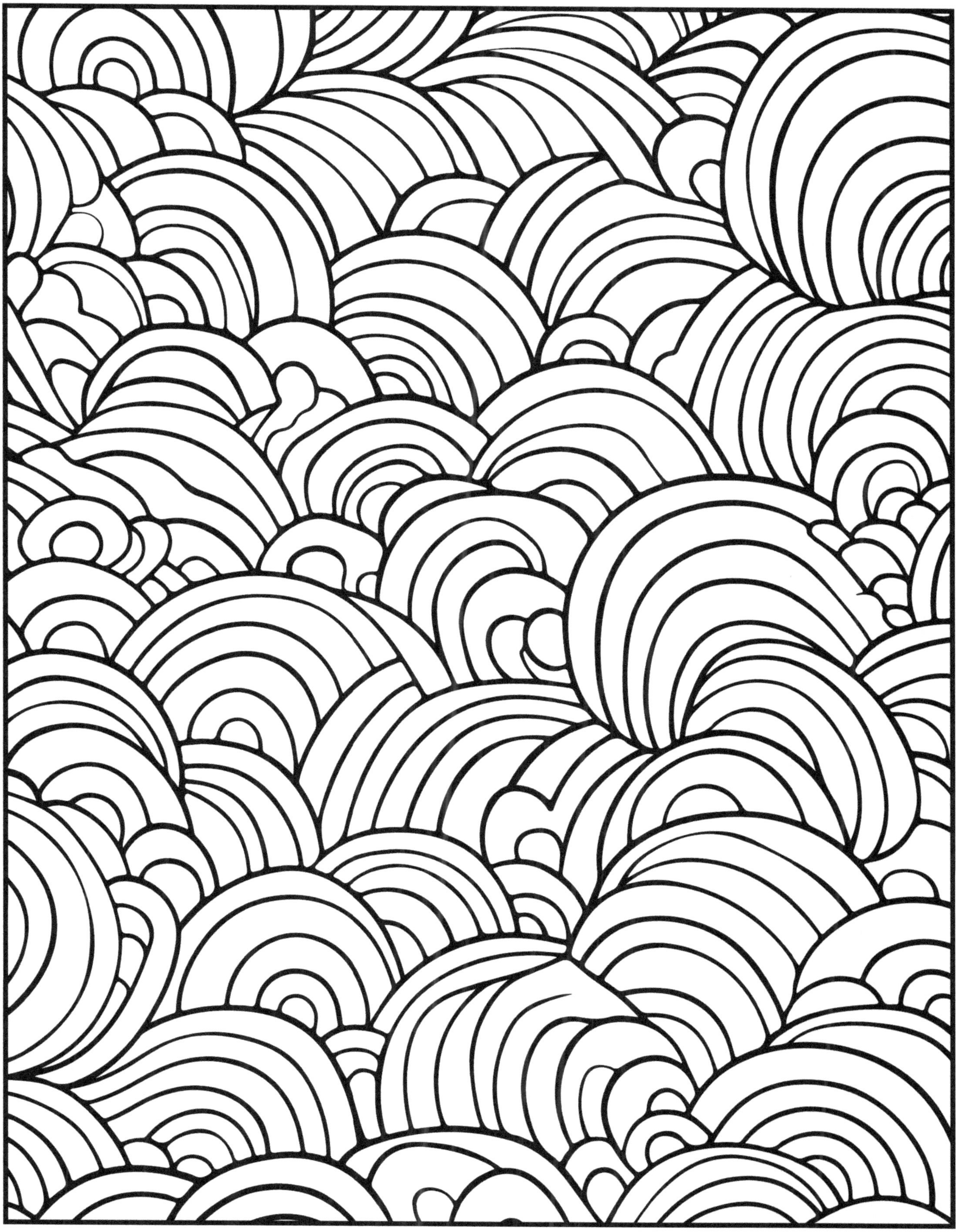

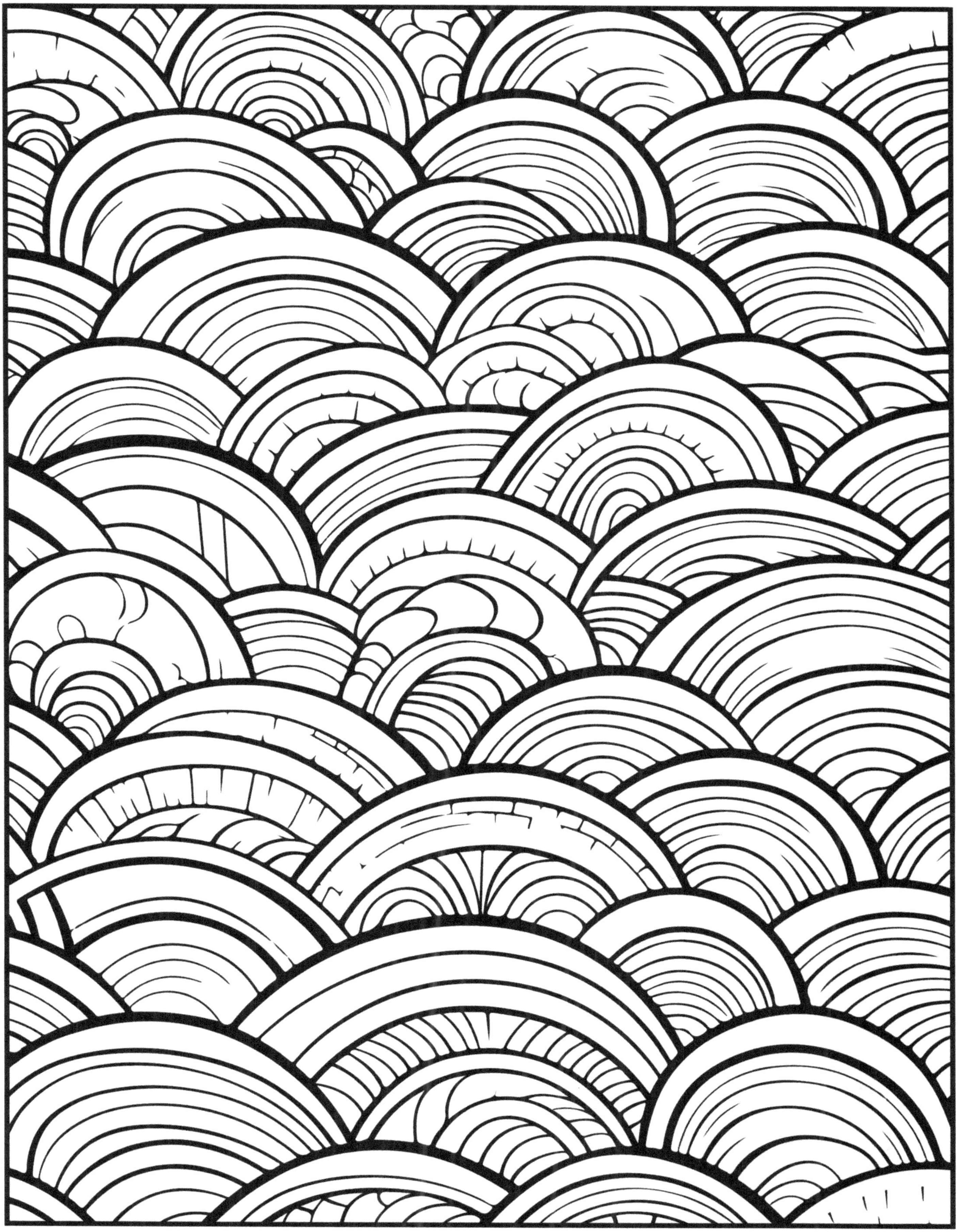

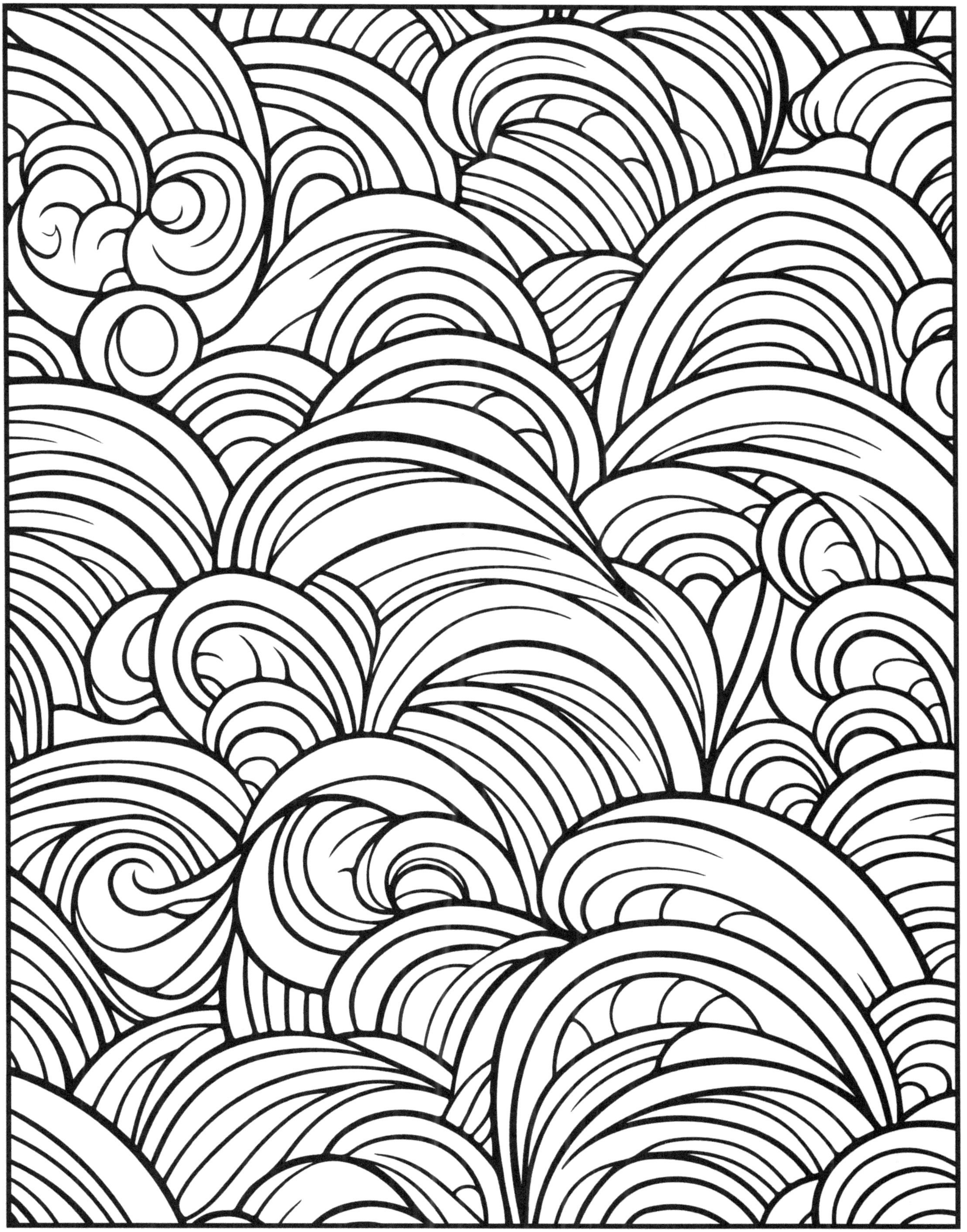

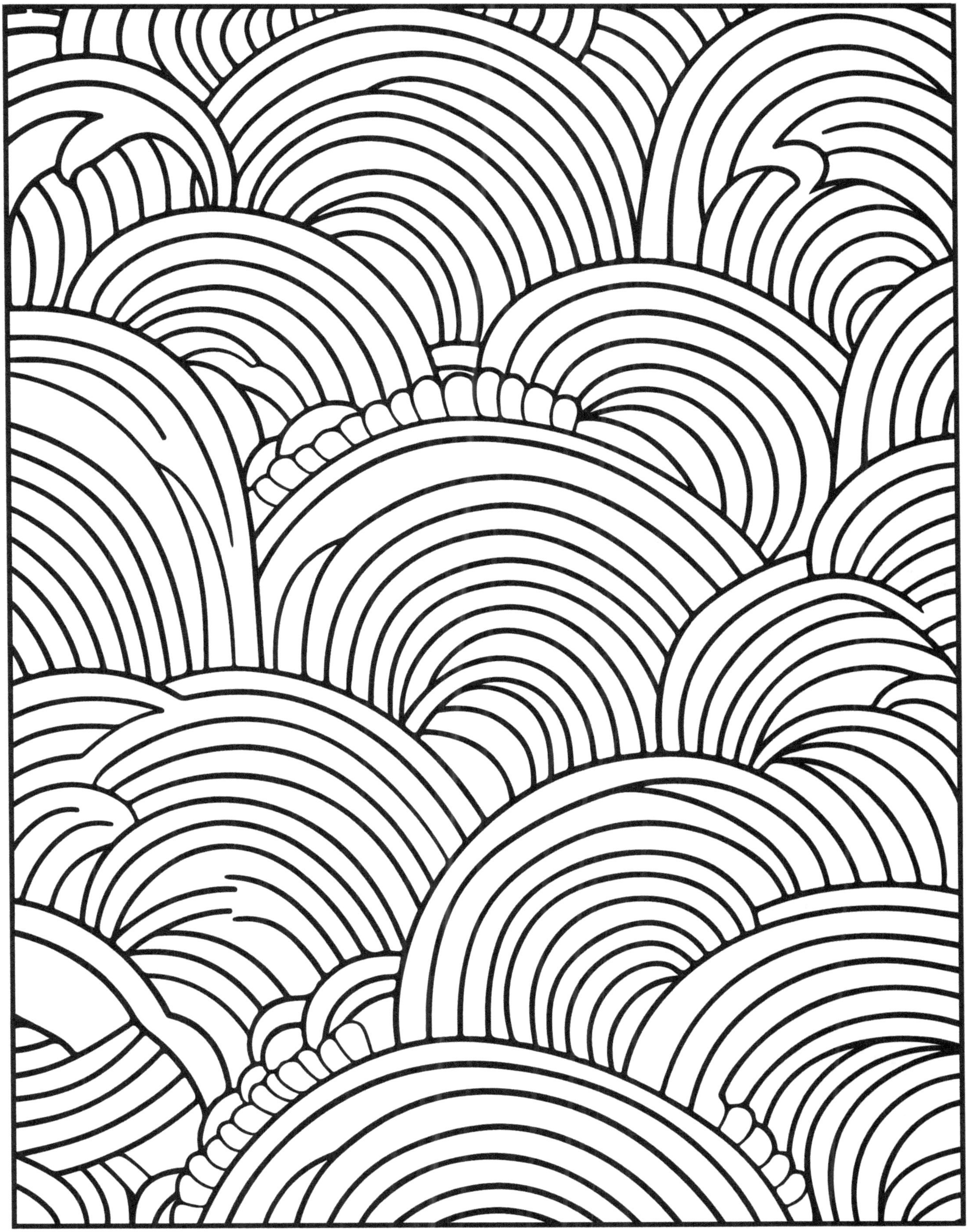

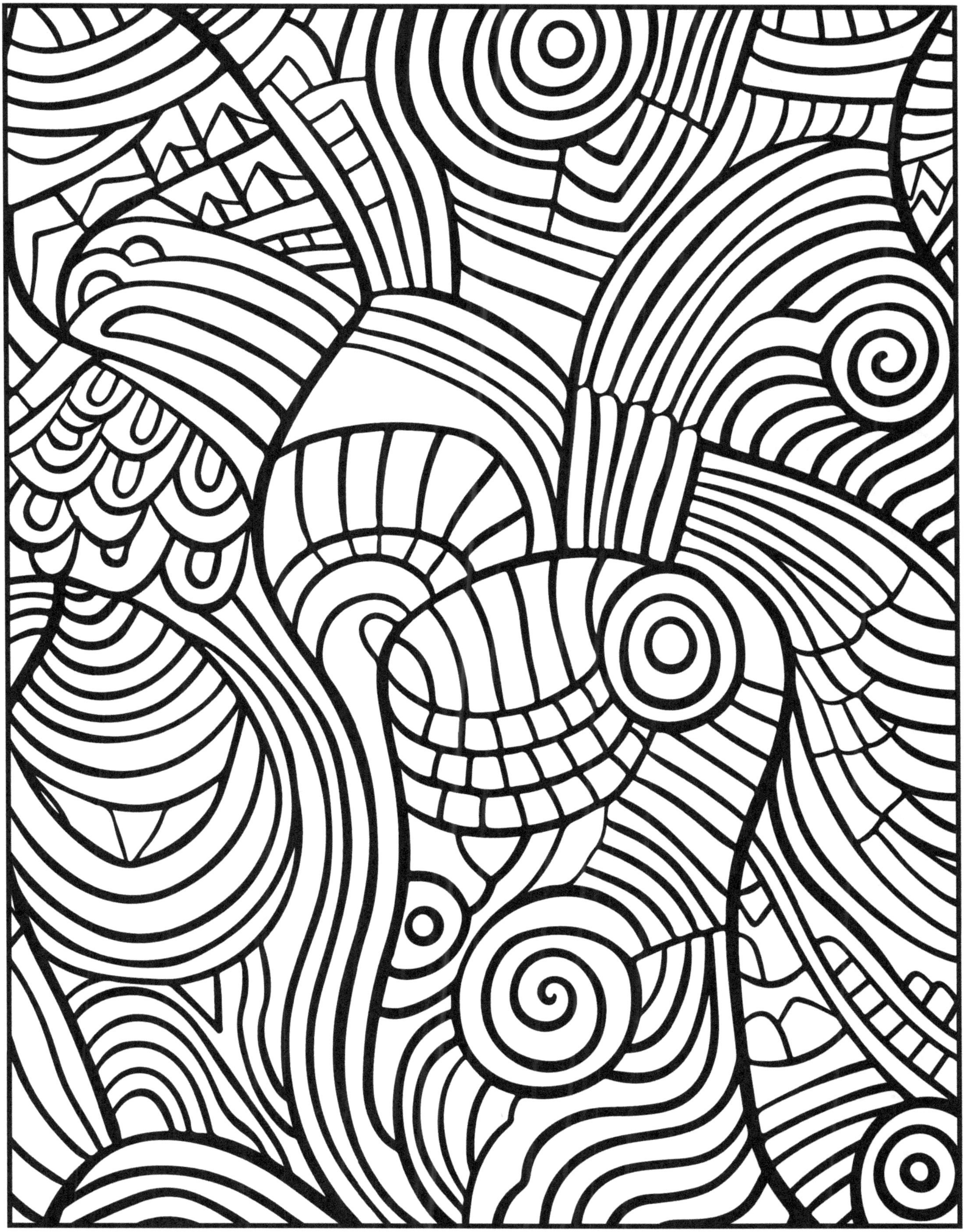

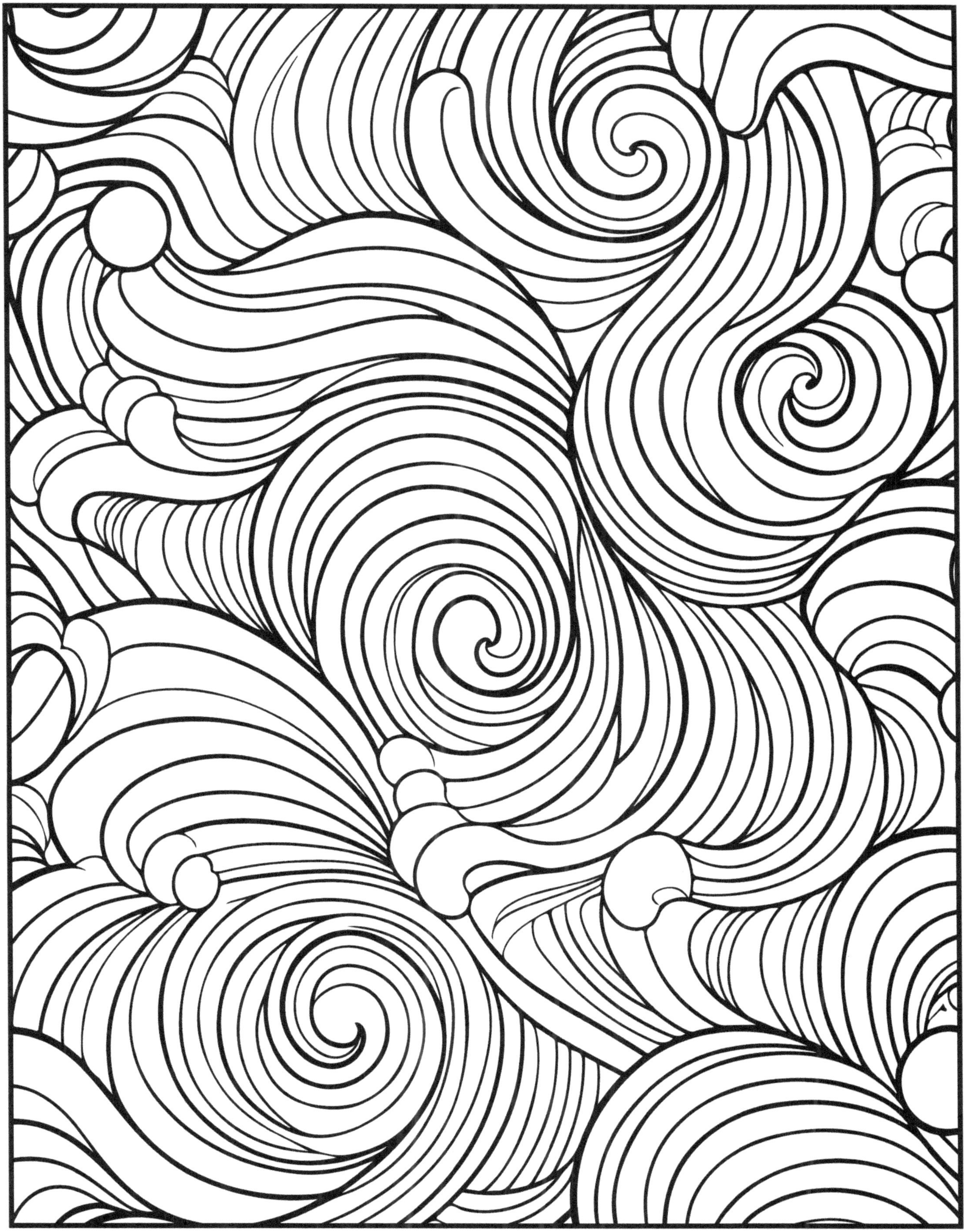

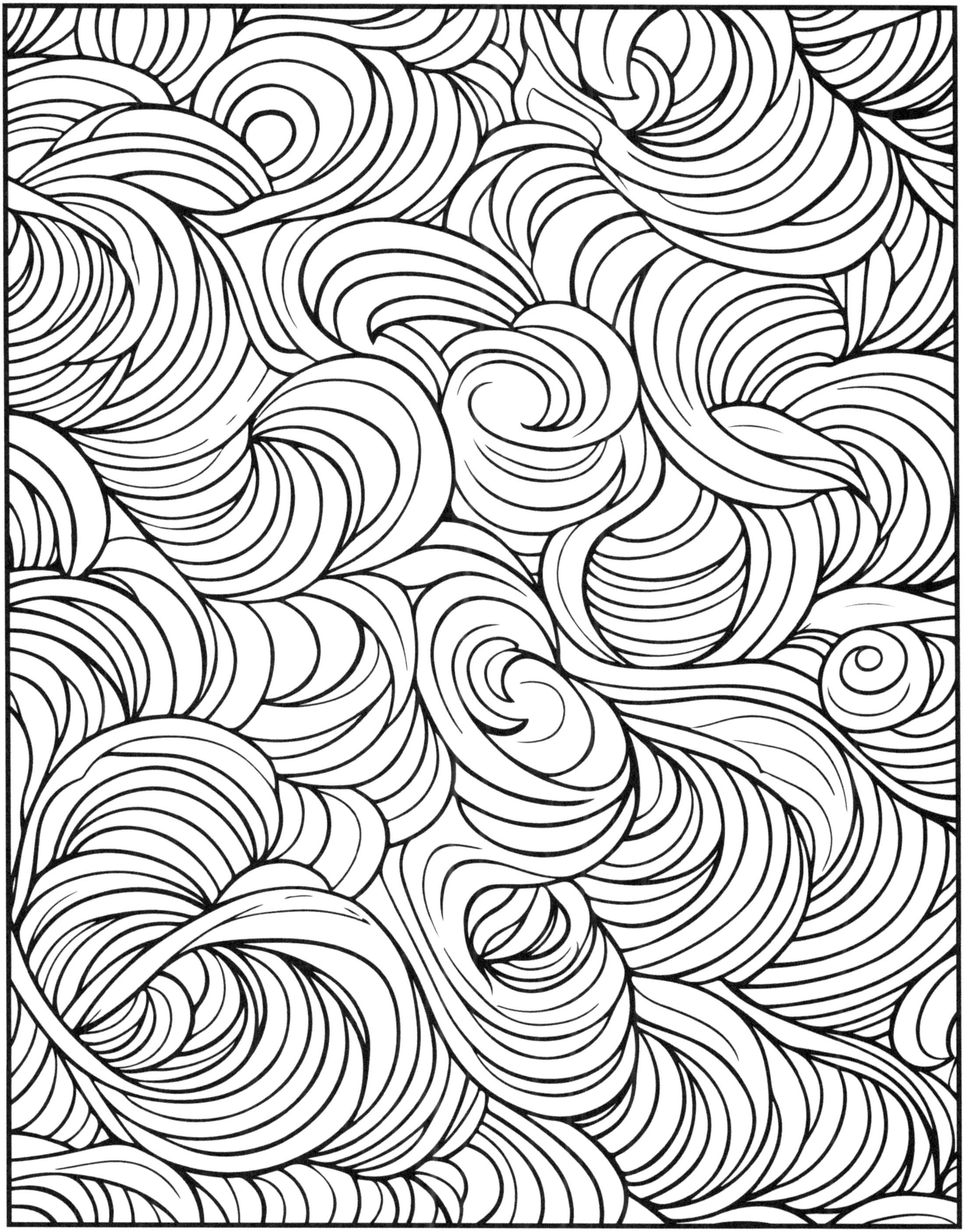

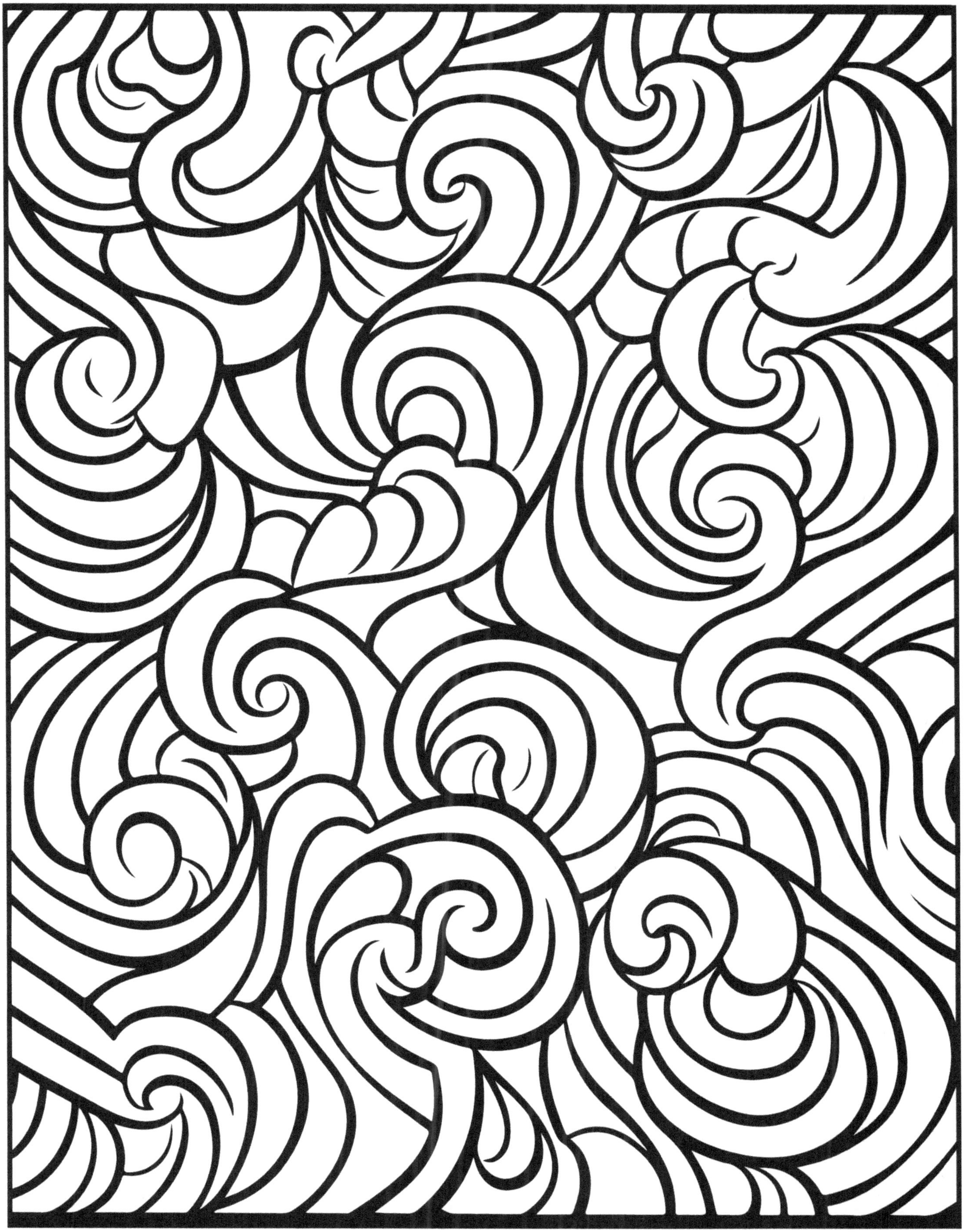

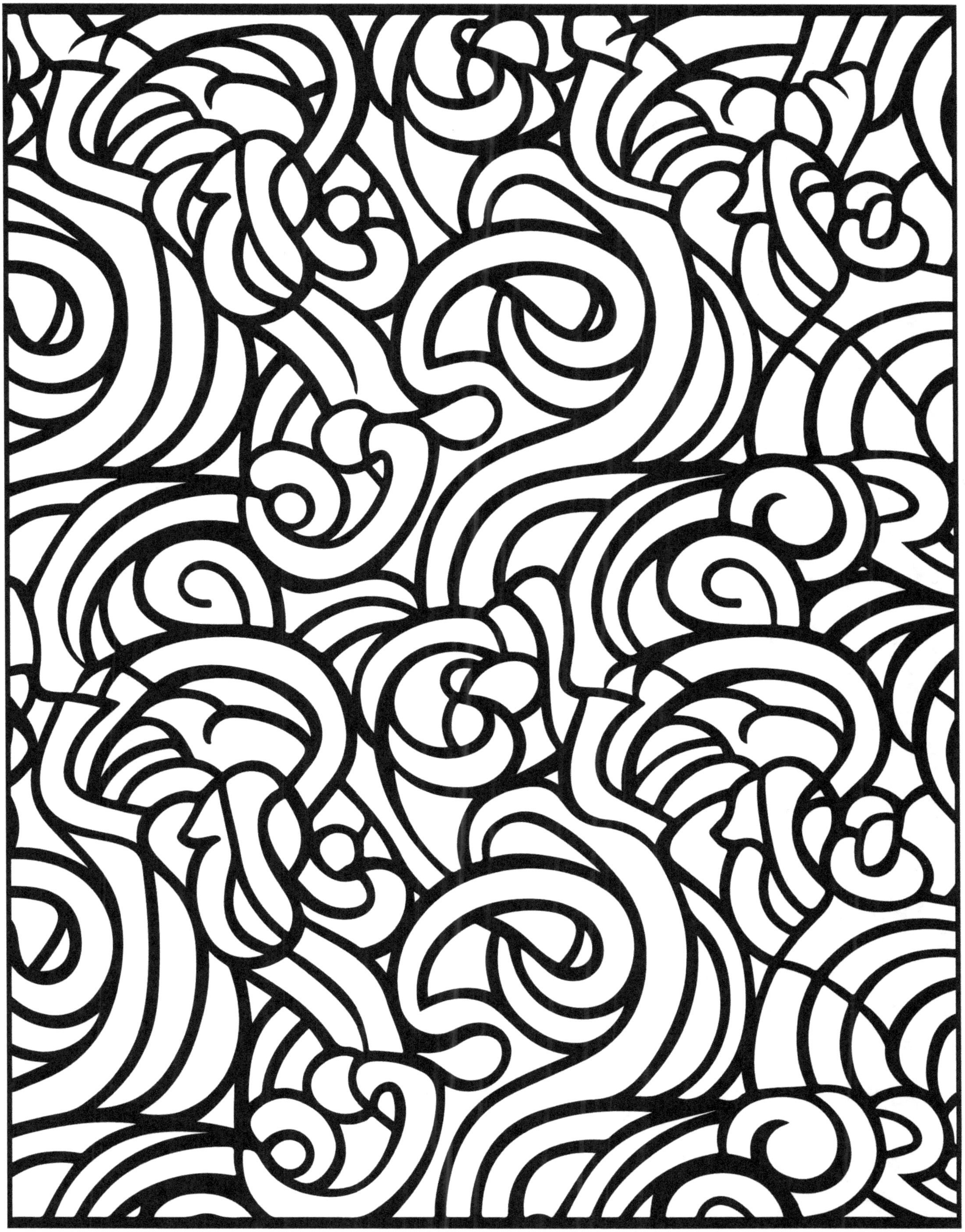

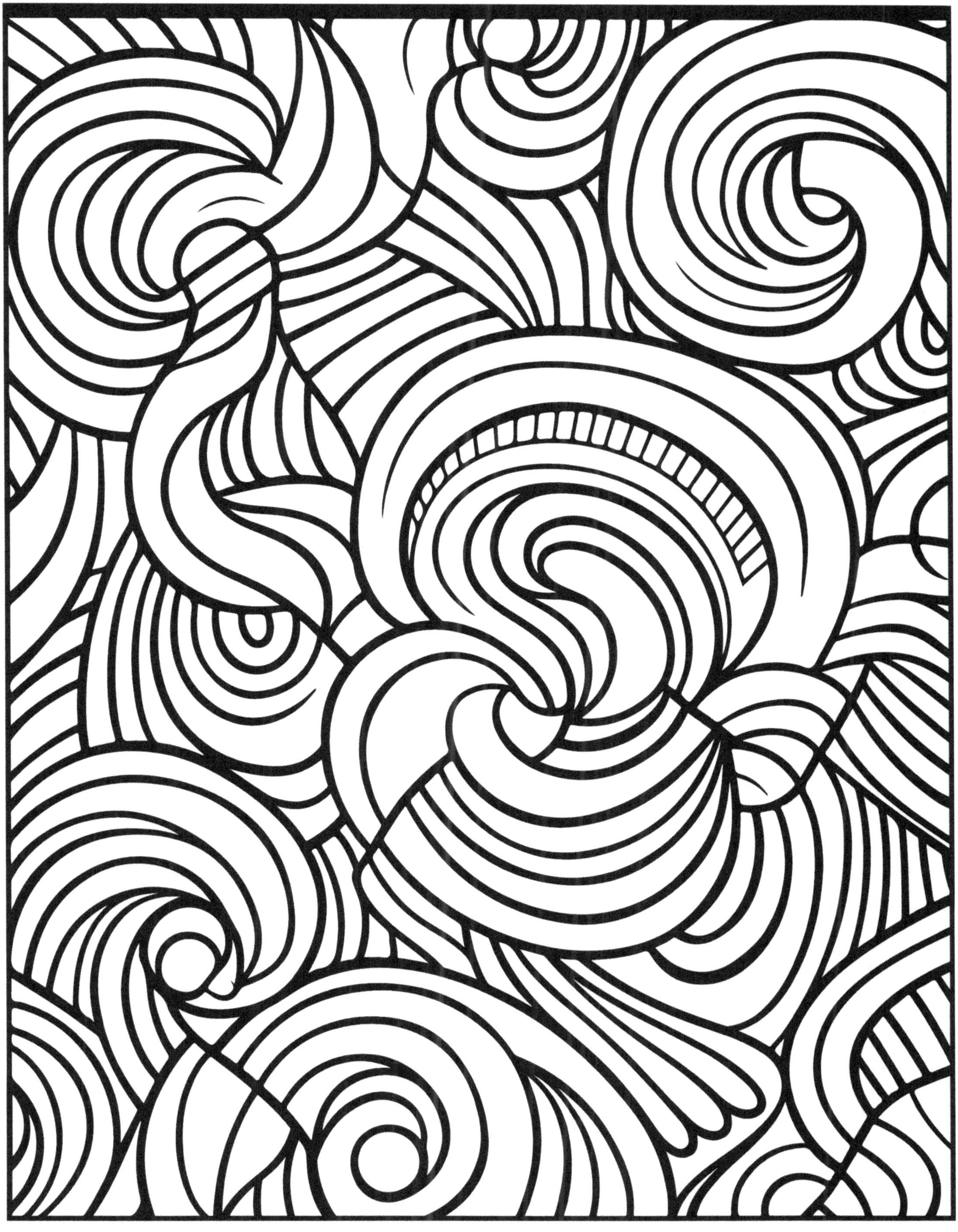

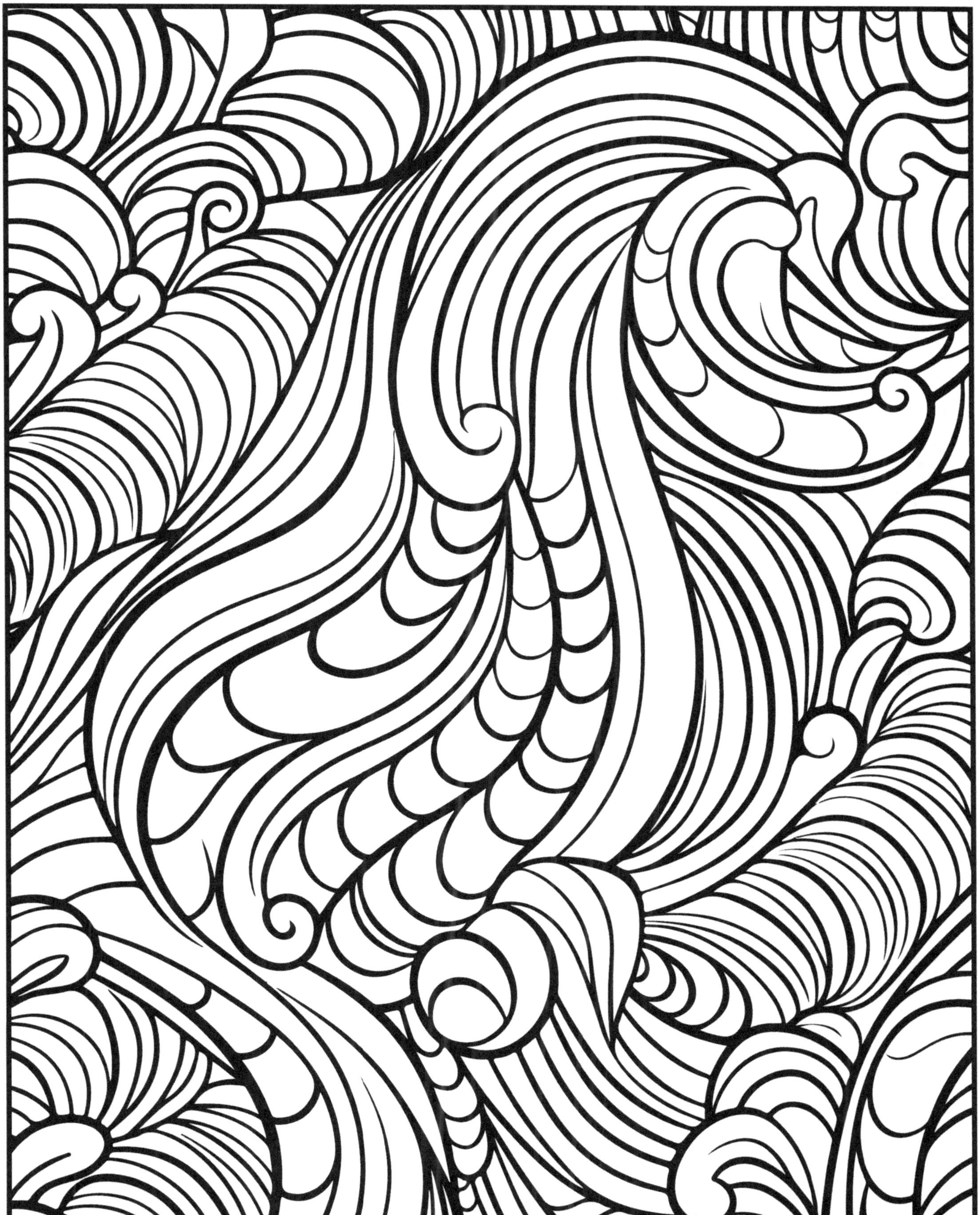

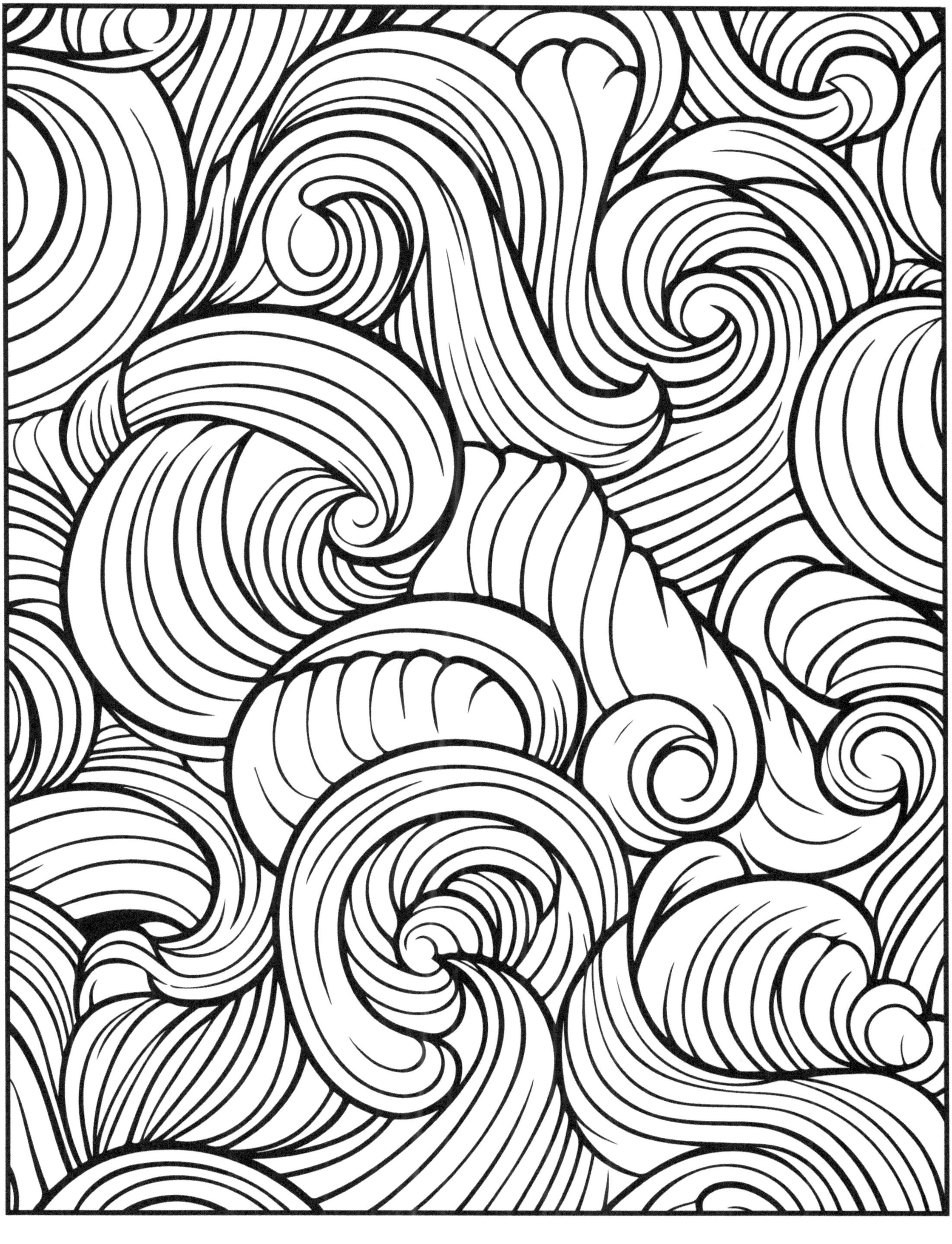

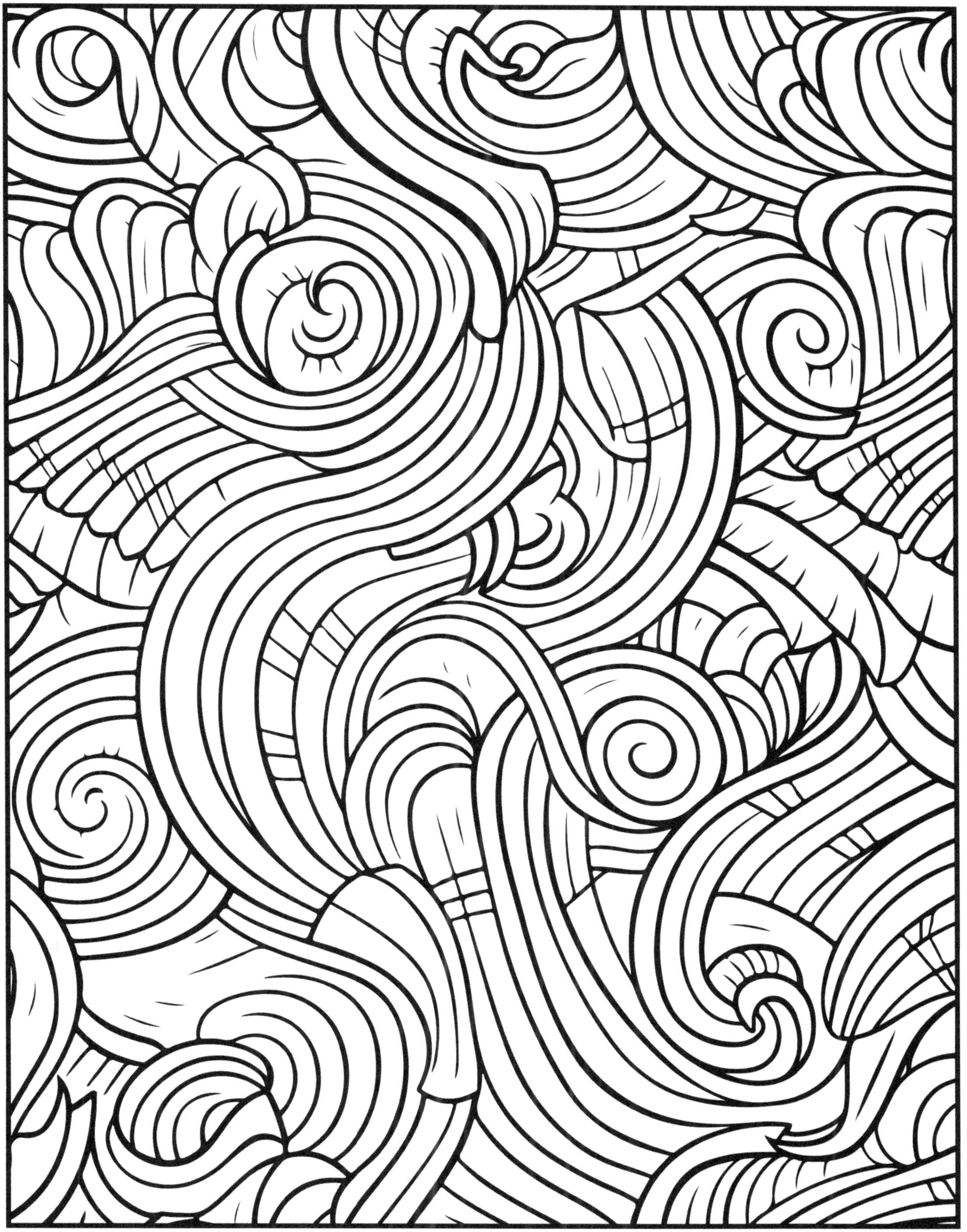

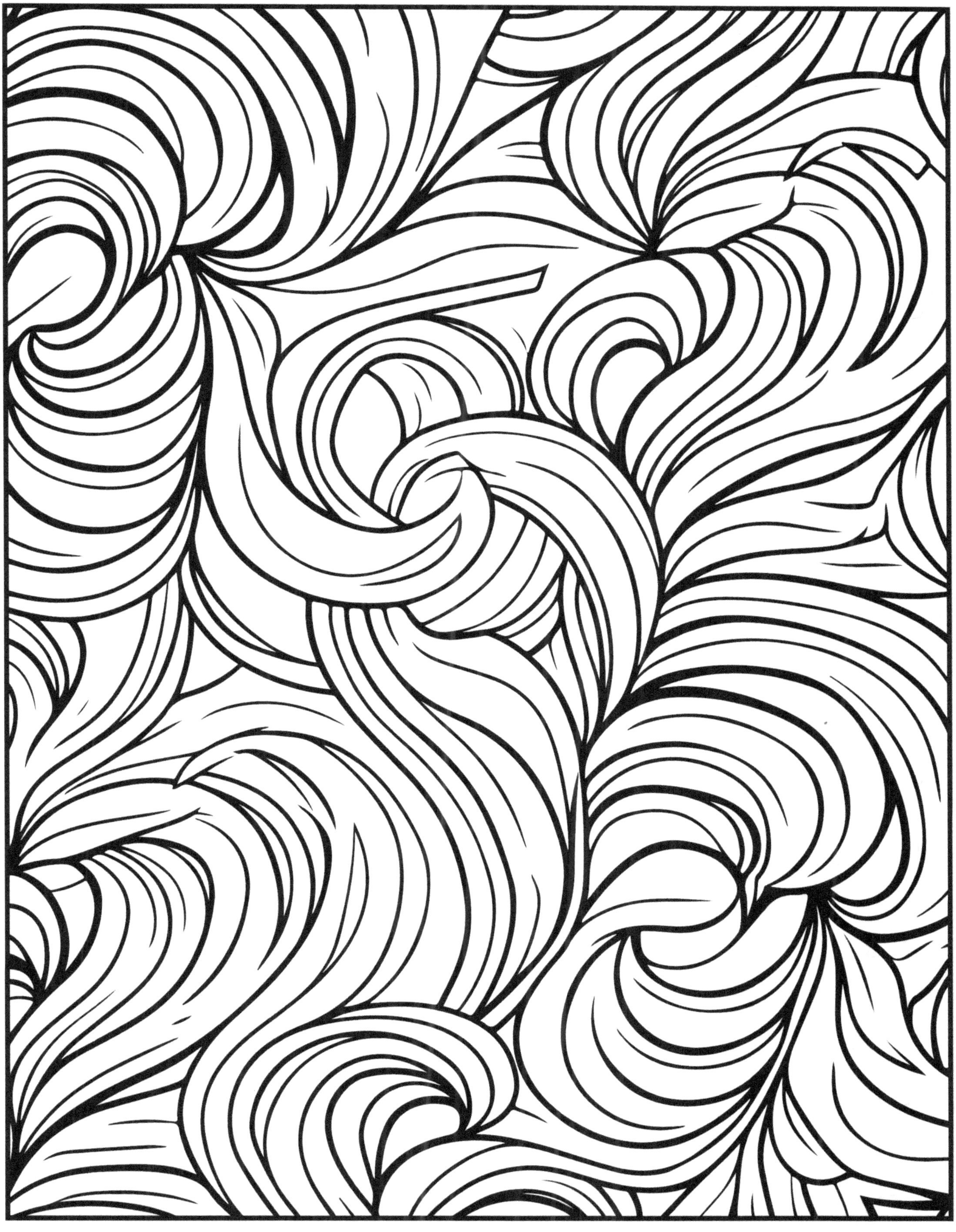

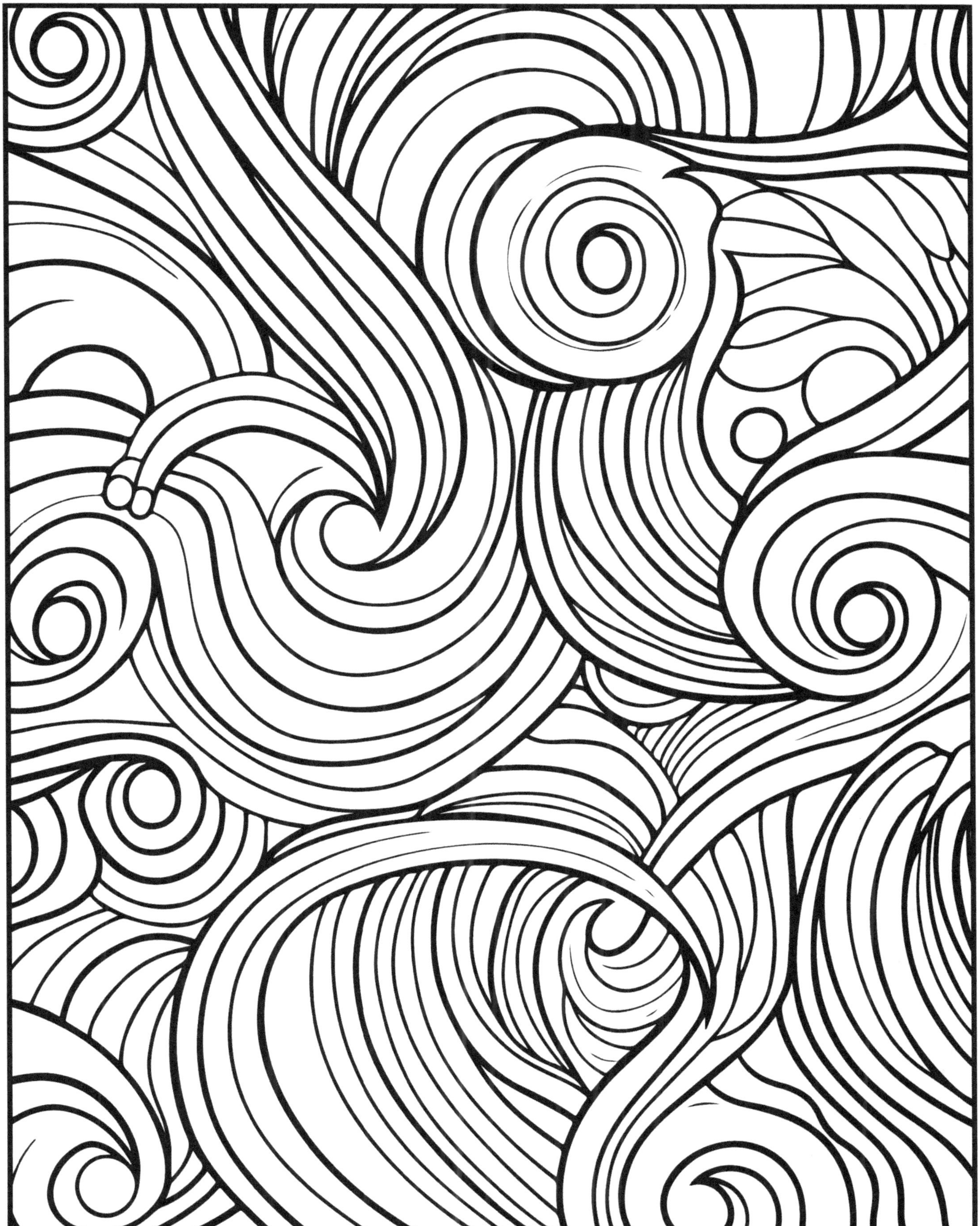

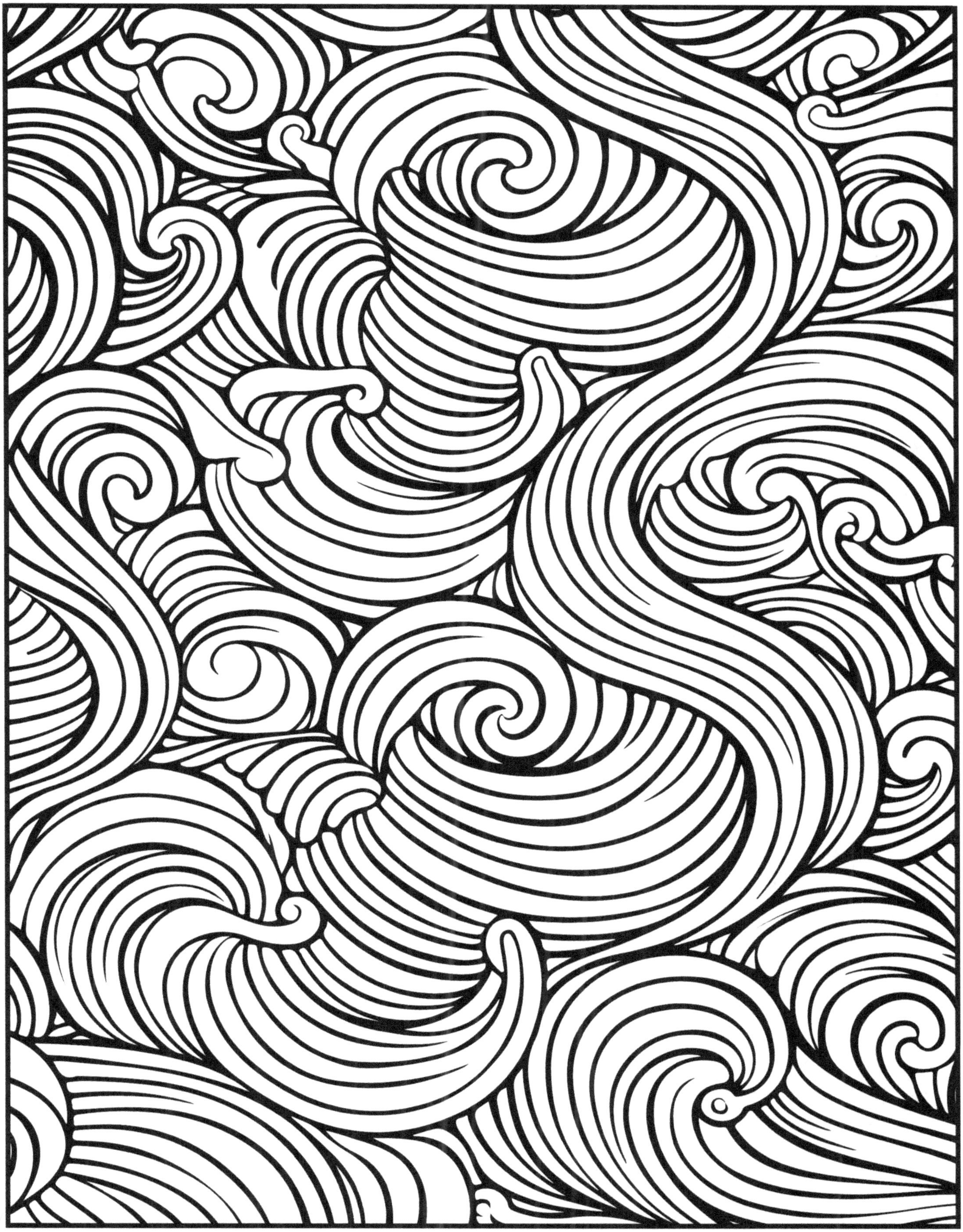

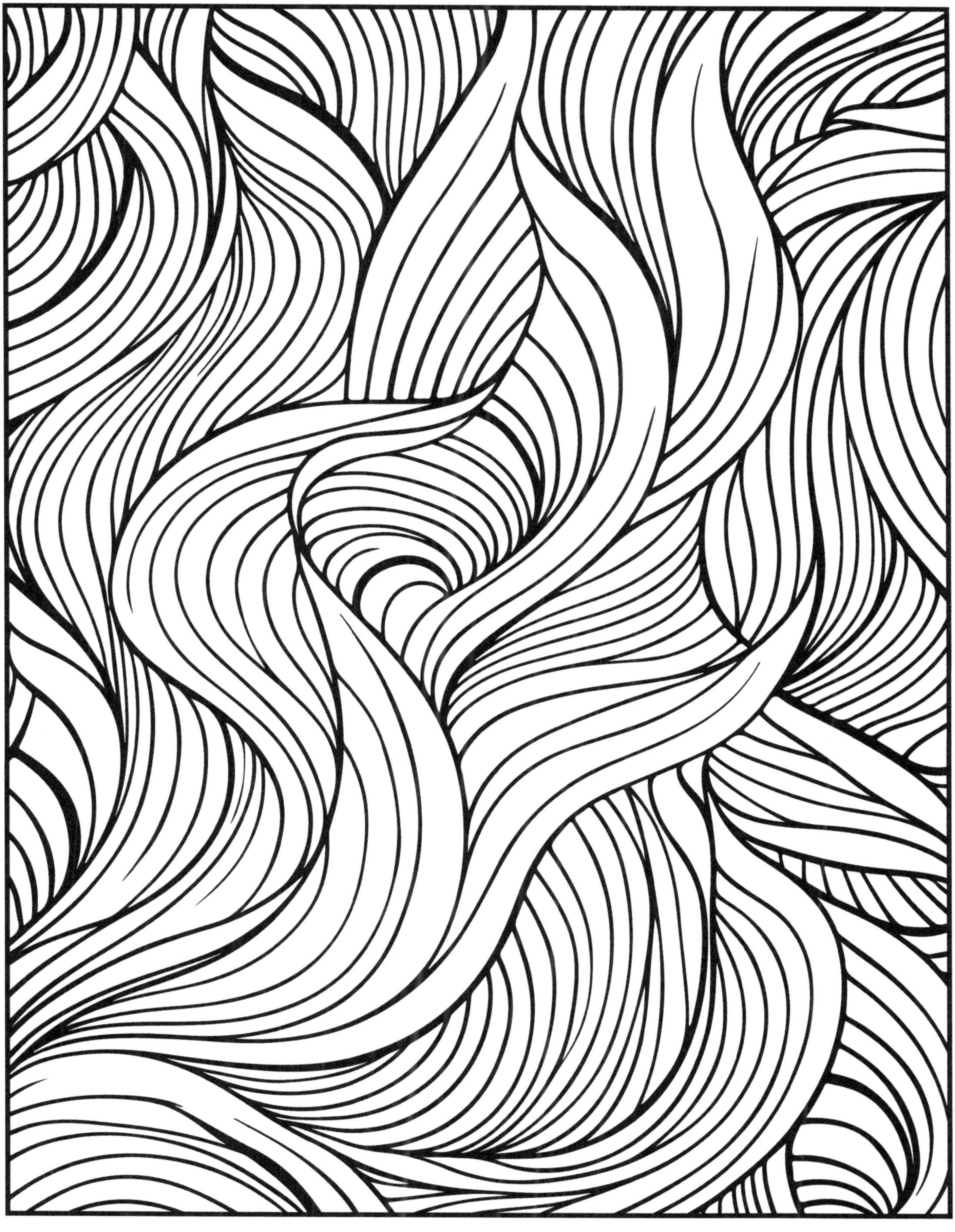

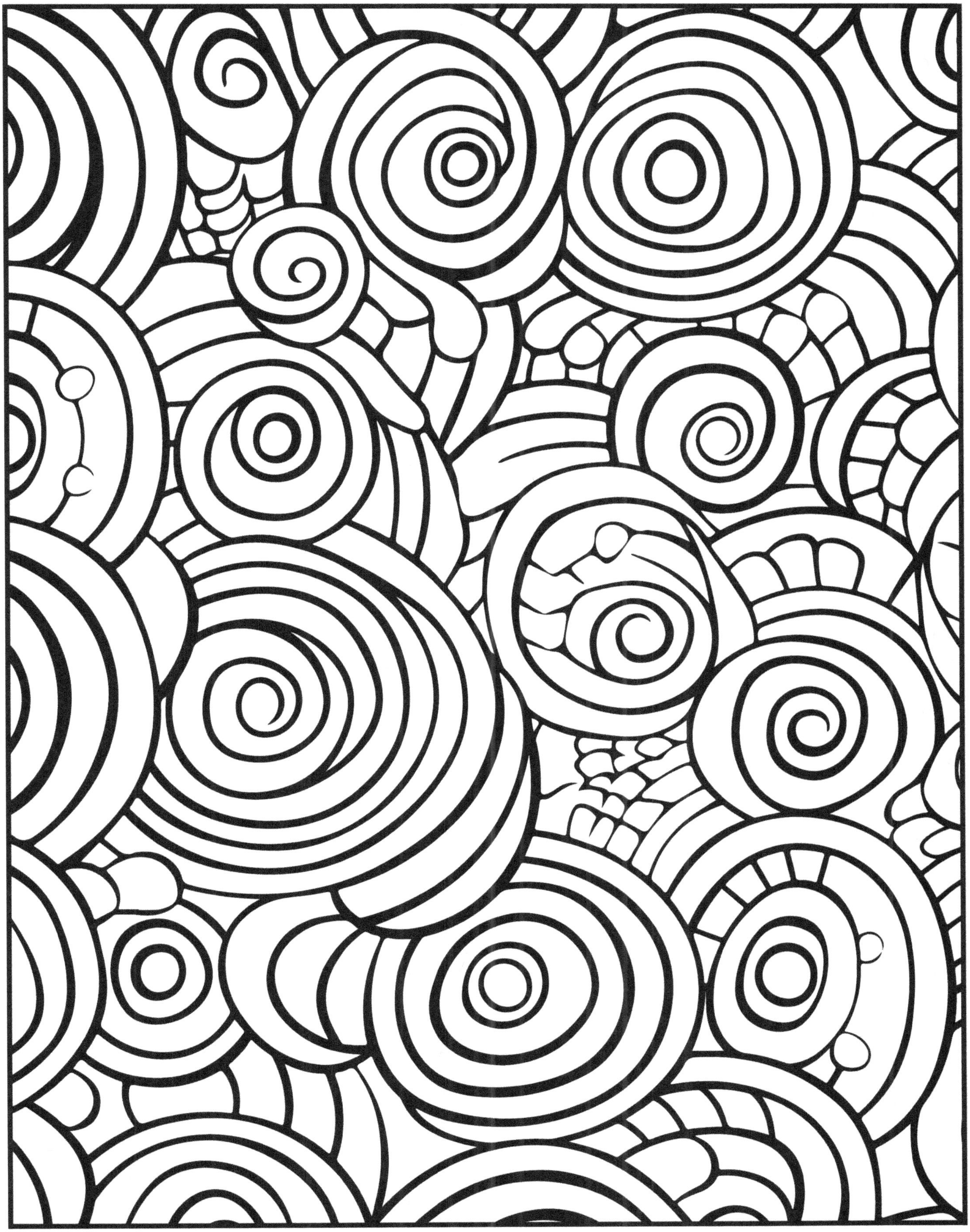

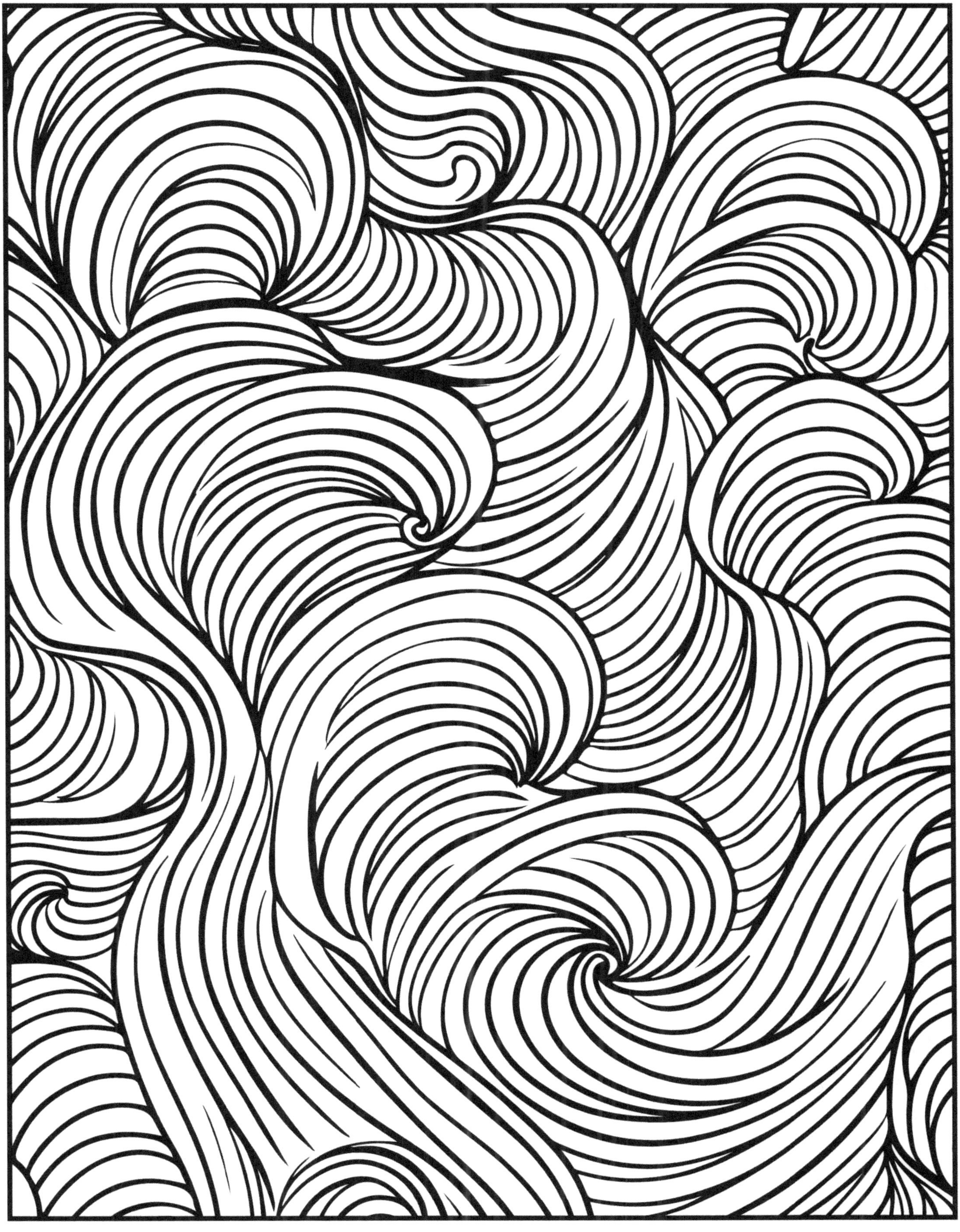

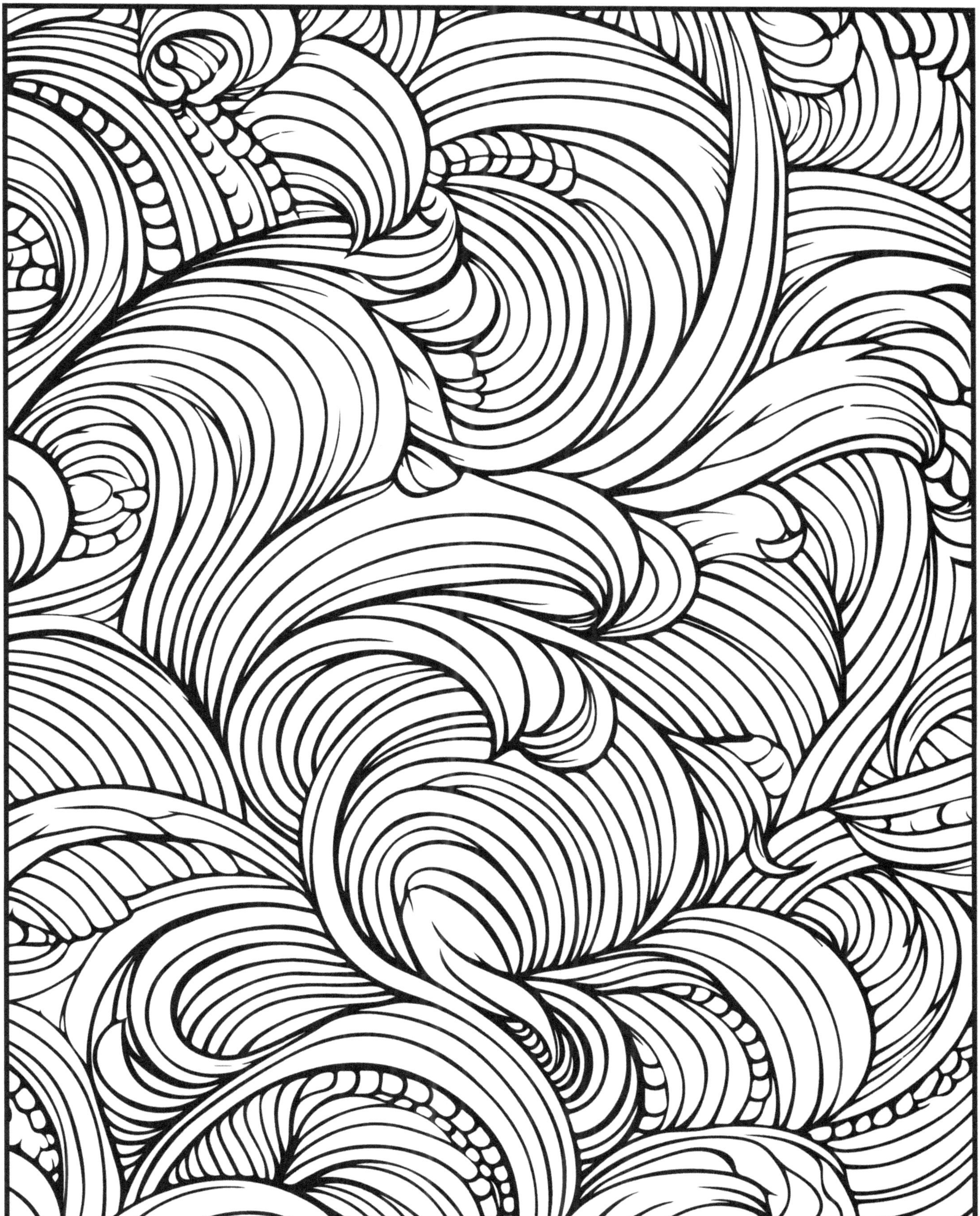

www.ingramcontent.com/pod-product-compliance
Lightning Source LLC
Chambersburg PA
CBHW082211220526
45470CB00010B/3127
* 9 7 9 8 3 2 7 5 8 9 7 6 6 *